# PRENTICE HALL
# WRITING AND GRAMMAR

## Reading Support Practice Book

**Grade Seven**

Boston, Massachusetts,
Upper Saddle River, New Jersey

ISBN 0-13-361698-3

2 3 4 5 6 7 8 9 10     10 09 08

# CONTENTS

Read the following passage. Then answer the questions that follow. Write the letter of the correct answer on the line at the right.

> My mother believed you could be anything you wanted to be in America. You could open a restaurant. You could work for the government and get good retirement. You could buy a house with almost no money down. You could become rich. You could become instantly famous.

[Amy Tan, "Two Kinds"]

1. Which statement best expresses the main idea of the passage?          1. _______
   A. My mother looked forward to retirement.
   B. My mother wanted to buy a house with almost no money down.
   C. My mother believed you could be anything you wanted to be in America.
   D. My mother felt that the American dream was only a folk tale.

2. What does the suffix *-ment* mean in *government* and *retirement?*          2. _______
   A. in the manner of          C. something written
   B. science, study          D. action, process

Read the following passage. Then answer the questions that follow. Write the letter of the correct answer on the line at the right.

> The corridor I was in began angling left and slanting downward and I thought that was wrong, but I kept on walking. All I could hear was the empty sound of my own footsteps and I didn't pass a soul. Then I heard that sort of hollow roar ahead that means open space and people talking. The tunnel turned sharp left; I went down a short flight of stairs and came out on the third level of Grand Central Station. For just a moment I thought I was back on the second level, but I saw the room was smaller, there were fewer ticket windows and train gates, and the information booth in the center was wood and old-looking. And the man in the booth wore a green eyeshade and long black sleeve protectors. Then I saw why; there were open-flame gaslights.

[Jack Finney, "The Third Level"]

3. Which one of the following words does *not* rhyme with *thought?*          3. _______
   A. bought          B. through          C. caught          D. fought

4. How should the word *information* be divided into syllables?          4. _______
   A. infor-ma-tion          C. in-for-ma-tion
   B. in-form-a-tion          D. in-for-ma-ti-on

5. Which item best describes the author's purpose and point of view in the          5. _______
   passage?
   A. to entertain; first person
   B. to persuade; first person
   C. to describe; third person
   D. to inform; third person

Read the following passage. Then answer the questions that follow. Write the letter of the correct answer on the line at the right.

> From then on he understood that he had to perform only to the standards he had established for himself. There was never any parental pressure on Tiger to win; anything was an acceptable outcome as long as an appropriate effort was made to avoid losing. Once, his effort failed to measure up, a mistake compounded by the fact that his father was a witness: At the Orange Bowl Junior Classic in Miami, Tiger was leading when he missed a short putt, which ignited a short fuse. He sulked the rest of the round, losing his lead and eventually the tournament. It was apparent that he had quit on himself, the one mistake Earl would not tolerat....

[John Strege, *Tiger: A Biography of Tiger Woods*]

**6.** From context clues in the passage, how would you define *ignite?*     6. ______
   **A.** set fire to     **B.** cut     **C.** extinguish     **D.** inflate

**7.** The word *pressure* contains the Latin root *press-*, which means to push steadily     7. ______
   against or press. All the words in the group below also contain this root *except*
   **A.** oppress     **B.** compress     **C.** repress     **D.** present

**8.** How should the word *apparent* be divided into syllables?     8. ______
   **A.** ap-par-ent     **B.** a-ppar-ent     **C.** ap-pa-rent     **D.** ap-pare-nt

**9.** Which statement below is the best paraphrase of the first sentence in the passage?     9. ______
   **A.** He understood then that standards were not important.
   **B.** He understood then that he had to live up to the standards he set for himself.
   **C.** He understood that different people had different standards.
   **D.** From then on he realized he would have to change his standards.

Read the following passage. Then answer the questions that follow. Write the letter of the correct answer on the line at the right.

> My mother made all the clothes we wore, even my brothers' overalls. She made all the towels and sheets we used. She spent the summers canning vegetables and fruits. She spent the winter evenings making quilts enough to cover all our beds.

[Alice Walker, "In Search of Our Mothers' Gardens"]

**10.** Which statement below best expresses the implied main idea of the passage?     10. ______
   **A.** My mother was better at canning than at quilting.
   **B.** My mother worked hard to supply what our family needed.
   **C.** My mother worked harder in summer than in winter.
   **D.** When we were children, we all helped our mother.

Read the following passage. Then answer the questions that follow. Write the letter of the correct answer on the line at the right.

> My children are upstairs in the house next door, having dinner with the Ecuadorian family that lives on the top floor. The father speaks some English, the mother less than that. The two daughters are fluent in both their native and their adopted languages, but the youngest child, a son, a close friend of my two boys, speaks almost no Spanish. This doesn't surprise me; it was the way my mother was raised, American among Italians.

[Anna Quindlen, "Melting Pot"]

**11.** What does the suffix *-est* mean in *youngest?*    11. ______
   **A.** not        **B.** most        **C.** state, quality        **D.** before

**12.** From context clues in the passage, how would you define *fluent?*    12. ______
   **A.** able to write or speak easily or smoothly
   **B.** vague or mysterious
   **C.** doubtful, hesitant
   **D.** overly talkative

**13.** Which conclusion below can you draw from the passage?    13. ______
   **A.** The writer has never been to Ecuador.
   **B.** The two boys get along with the neighbors' son but not with their daughters.
   **C.** The writer does not like having her children visit the neighbors.
   **D.** The writer is of Italian ancestry on her mother's side.

Read the following passage. Then answer the questions that follow. Write the letter of the correct answer on the line at the right.

> Rip Van Winkle, however, was one of those happy mortals, of foolish, well-oiled dispositions, who take the world easy, eat white bread or brown, whichever can be got with least thought or trouble, and would rather starve on a penny than work for a pound.[11] If left to himself, he would have whistled life away in perfect contentment; but his wife kept continually dinning in his ears about his idleness, his carelessness, and the ruin he was bringing on his family. Morning, noon, and night, her tongue was incessantly going, and everything he said or did was sure to produce a torrent of household eloquence.

---
**11. pound:** British unit of money.

[Washington Irving, "Rip Van Winkle"]

**14.** Which item below best expresses the contrast shown in the passage?    14. ______
   **A.** between Rip's easygoing personality and his wife's scolding
   **B.** between Rip's personality and his occupation
   **C.** between work and play
   **D.** between poverty and wealth

NAME _______________________________________________     DATE _______________

15. Which of the following is the best summary of the passage?     15. ______
    A. Rip Van Winkle was forced to listen to his wife's scolding morning, noon,
       and night.
    B. Rip Van Winkle was a careless, idle person.
    C. Rip Van Winkle was easygoing by nature, and his wife constantly scolded
       him for idleness.
    D. Rip Van Winkle's laziness brought his family to the edge of ruin.

Read the following passage. Then answer the questions that follow. Write the letter
of the correct answer on the line at the right.

> I looked again. It was a sad thing to behold. This wonderful little creature of
> summertime in the big rough hand of the old peasant. Here it was in the cold
> of winter, absolutely helpless and pathetic, not suspended in a shaft of summer
> light, not the most alive thing in the world, but the most helpless and
> heartbreaking.

[William Saroyan, "The Hummingbird That Lived Through Winter"]

16. Which statement below best expresses the implied main idea of the passage?     16. ______
    A. The old peasant's hand was big and rough.
    B. The wonderful little bird looked helpless and sad in the cold of winter.
    C. The winter that year was especially cold.
    D. The little bird should have lived through the winter but did not.

17. In which word is the *gh* letter combination pronounced differently from the     17 ______
    way it is pronounced in *rough?*
    A. tough          B. laugh          C. thought          D. trough

18. The word *pathetic* contains the Greek root *-path-*, which also appears in the     18. ______
    words *sympathy* and *pathology*. Which item below best defines the meaning of
    *pathetic*?
    A. curious                  C. arousing pity or sorrow
    B. inspiring fear or awe     D. amusing

Read the following passage. Then answer the questions that follow. Write the letter
of the correct answer on the line at the right.

> That stretching sound you hear is attitudes about women athletes continuing
> to expand. After the 1996 Atlanta Summer Olympics and now the Nagano Games,
> it's clear that the U.S.'s female athletic heroes don't have to play what Billie Jean
> King has jokingly called the "good clothes sports"—figure skating, tennis and
> golf. Women never lacked the strength or will to compete in the grittier sports,
> just the opportunity. When they get the chance, they can produce stirring results.
> As the U.S. men's Olympic goalie, Mike Richter of the New York Rangers, said
> admiringly after watching the U.S. women play Canada, "You felt so good for
> them, the way they were just bleeding for each other to win every game."

[Johnette Howard, "Golden Girls: The 1998 U.S. Women's Hockey Team"]

NAME _______________________________________________ DATE ______________

**19.** Which statement below is the best paraphrase of the first sentence in the passage?  **19.** ______
    **A.** It will be a long time before attitudes about women athletes will change.
    **B.** Attitudes about women athletes continue to expand.
    **C.** Women's attitudes about sports are changing.
    **D.** Women's attitudes about sports are different from men's attitudes.

**20.** Which sports are jokingly called "good clothes sports" in the passage?  **20.** ______
    **A.** hockey, basketball, and golf
    **B.** hockey and baseball
    **C.** tennis and hockey
    **D.** figure skating, tennis, and golf

**21.** Which item below is the best statement of the main idea in the passage?  **21.** ______
    **A.** Until now, women have lacked the opportunity to participate in the grittier sports, such as hockey.
    **B.** Attitudes about women athletes are continuing to expand.
    **C.** Mike Richter, the U.S. men's Olympic goalie, admired the performance of the women's hockey team.
    **D.** The 1996 Atlanta Summer Olympics were not as significant as the Nagano Games for women athletes.

**22.** How would you describe the author's purpose in this passage?  **22.** ______
    **A.** to entertain         **C.** to describe
    **B.** to inform           **D.** to persuade

Read the following passage. Then answer the questions that follow. Write the letter of the correct answer on the line at the right.

> The swan instantly assumed great dignity and sailed out to the middle of the water, where it put itself to rights with much dabbling and preening, smoothing its feathers with little showers of drops. Mr. Peters waited, to make sure that it was all right and had suffered no damage in its struggles. Presently the swan, when it was satisfied with its appearance, floated in to the bank once more, and in a moment, instead of the great white bird, there was a little man all in green with a golden crown and a long beard, standing by the water. He had fierce glittering eyes and looked by no means friendly.
>
> [Joan Aiken, "The Third Wish"]

**23.** When did the swan float in to the bank again?  **23.** ______
    **A.** after Mr. Peters left the scene
    **B.** after the little man all in green appeared
    **C.** after it had preened and smoothed its feathers
    **D.** before it sailed out to the middle of the water

**24.** Some information in the passage is important and some is not important. Which information is unimportant?  **24.** ______
    **A.** The swan was suddenly transformed into a little man all in green.
    **B.** Mr. Peters waited to see if the swan had suffered no damage.
    **C.** The swan created little showers of drops when it preened itself.
    **D.** The little man in green did not look friendly.

Read the following passage. Then answer the questions that follow. Write the letter of the correct answer on the line at the right.

> All in all, it was not the finest broadcast CBS News has ever done. But the worst part came when I introduced the "end piece," a feature story that Hughes Rudd had done about raft racing on the Chatahoochie River.[3] Again, when I finished the introduction, I turned to the monitor and, again, nothing happened. Then, through the glass window of the "fishbowl," I heard a loud and plaintive wail. "What is going on?" screamed the fill-in executive producer. I could hear him perfectly clearly, and so could half of America. The microphone on my tie-clip was open.

3. **Chatahoochie River:** River running south through Georgia and forming part of the borders of Georgia, Alabama, and Florida.

[Charles Osgood, "Our Finest Hour"]

25. Which of the following states an *opinion* in the passage?          25. ______
    A. The broadcast was not the finest that CBS News has ever done.
    B. The narrator introduced the "end piece."
    C. Hughes Rudd had done a story about raft racing.
    D. The fill-in executive producer said, "What is going on?"

26. Which word below does *not* contain a sound that is the same as the sound          26. ______
    made by the *ph* in *microphone?*
    A. telephone     B. physics          C. import          D. off

Read the following passage. Then answer the questions that follow. Write the letter of the correct answer on the line at the right.

> They are the only ones who understand me. I am the only one who understands them. Four skinny trees with skinny necks and pointy elbows like mine. Four who do not belong here but are here. Four raggedy excuses planted by the city. From our room we can hear them, but Nenny just sleeps and doesn't appreciate these things.

[Sandra Cisneros, "Four Skinny Trees"]

27. What inference can you make about the narrator in this passage?          27. ______
    A. She does not like going to school.
    B. She feels lonely and misunderstood.
    C. She loves all kinds of trees.
    D. She has just had a fight with Nenny.

     

Read the following passage. Then answer the questions that follow. Write the letter of the correct answer on the line at the right.

> At the end of August, Justin got a break. A neighbor wrote a letter to the local newspaper describing Justin's project, and an editor thought it would make a good story. One day a reporter entered the Lebo garage. Stepping gingerly through the tires and frames that covered the floor, she found a boy with cut fingers and dirty nails, banging a seat onto a frame. His clothes were covered with grease. In her admiring article about a boy who was devoting his summer to help kids he didn't even know, she said Justin needed bikes and money, and she printed his home phone number.

[Phillip Hoose, "Justin Lebo"]

28. Which statement below is an *opinion,* rather than a *fact*?  28. ______
   A. The reporter entered the Lebo garage.
   B. Justin's clothes were covered with grease.
   C. The editor thought an article about Justin would be a good story.
   D. A neighbor wrote a letter to the local newspaper describing Justin's project.

29. When did the reporter arrive at the Lebo garage?  29. ______
   A. before a neighbor wrote a letter to the newspaper
   B. after she saw Justin banging a seat onto a frame
   C. after a neighbor wrote a letter to the newspaper
   D. at the beginning of August

Read the following passage. Then answer the questions that follow. Write the letter of the correct answer on the line at the right.

> The fighters changed from their street clothes into fighting gear. Antonio wore white trunks, black socks, and black shoes. Felix wore sky blue trunks, red socks, and white boxing shoes. Each had dressing gowns to match their fighting trunks with their names neatly stitched on the back.

[Piri Thomas, "Amigo Brothers"]

30. What contrast does the writer draw between Antonio and Felix?  30. ______
   A. between their clothing and shoes
   B. between their dressing gowns
   C. between their height and weight
   D. between their attitudes

Read the following passage. Then answer the questions that follow. Write the letter of the correct answer on the line at the right.

> Sometimes I forget that part—talking to my child. Actually *being* with him. When I'm in charge of the kid, I tend to either stare at him like he's television or drift totally into a world of my own, running through my list of things-I-have-to-do-later-when-I'm-not-taking-care-of-the-kid. Or I take the job *so* seriously I become blinded by the severity of the responsibility, and panic. What I seem to miss is the middle ground—the part where you share, teach, learn, play—the part you can actually enjoy.

[Paul Reiser, "Stepping Out With My Baby"]

**31.** Which inference below can you make from the passage?    **31.** _______
    **A.** The writer is a busy professional with little time for children.
    **B.** The writer wishes he could find the middle ground and enjoy being a parent more.
    **C.** The writer is a bad parent.
    **D.** The writer spends a lot of time with his child.

**32.** The contrast the writer draws in the passage relates to    **32.** _______
    **A.** the difference between sharing and teaching
    **B.** the two extremes of withdrawing into his own world and taking the job so seriously that he panics
    **C.** the difference between good behavior and bad behavior
    **D.** his approach to being a parent, as opposed to his wife's approach

Read the following passage. Then answer the questions that follow. Write the letter of the correct answer on the line at the right.

> It is the hardest thing in the world to frighten a mongoose, because he is eaten up from nose to tail with curiosity. The motto of all the mongoose family is, "Run and find out"; and Rikki-tikki was a true mongoose. He looked at the cotton wool, decided that it was not good to eat, ran all round the table, sat up and put his fur in order, scratched himself, and jumped on the small boy's shoulder.

[Rudyard Kipling, "Rikki-tikki-tavi"]

**33.** What generalization can you form from the passage?    **33.** _______
    **A.** Rikki-tikki's behavior was unusual for a mongoose.
    **B.** Curiosity is the trademark of the mongoose family.
    **C.** Small children are often afraid of mongooses.
    **D.** Cotton wool is not good to eat.

    

**NAME** _______________________________     **DATE** ___________

Use this chart to answer the following questions.

**Outer Planets of the Solar System**

| Planet | Period of Revolution Around the Sun | Mass (Earth = 1) | Diameter (Earth = 1) |
|---|---|---|---|
| Mars | 687 days | 0.11 | 0.53 |
| Jupiter | 12 years | 317.89 | 11.19 |
| Saturn | 29 years | 95.15 | 9.44 |
| Uranus | 84 years | 14.54 | 4.10 |
| Neptune | 165 years | 17.23 | 3.88 |
| Pluto | 248 years | approx. 0.002 | 0.18 |

**34.** According to the chart, which planet takes 12 years to complete a revolution around the sun?   **34.** ______
    **A.** Mars                **C.** Uranus
    **B.** Jupiter             **D.** Neptune

**35.** Which are the only two planets listed that have a smaller diameter than Earth?   **35.** ______
    **A.** Mars and Saturn         **C.** Uranus and Neptune
    **B.** Jupiter and Pluto         **D.** Mars and Pluto

Read the following passage. Then answer the questions that follow. Write the letter of the correct answer on the line at the right.

> The person who called himself Lemon Brown peered forward, and Greg could see him clearly. He was an old man. His black, heavily wrinkled face was surrounded by a halo of crinkly white hair and whiskers that seemed to separate his head from the layers of dirty coats piled on his smallish frame. His pants were bagged to the knee, where they were met with rags that went down to the old shoes. The rags were held on with strings, and there was a rope around his middle. Greg relaxed. He had seen the man before, picking through the trash on the corner and pulling clothes out of a Salvation Army box.
>
> [Walter Dean Myers, "The Treasure of Lemon Brown"]

**36.** What conclusion can you draw from this passage?   **36.** ______
    **A.** Greg is not afraid of Lemon Brown.
    **B.** Lemon Brown is in disguise.
    **C.** Greg has never seen Lemon Brown before.
    **D.** Lemon Brown is surprised to see Greg.

**37.** Which item below is the best summary of the passage?          37. ______
   **A.** Lemon Brown was an old, ferocious-looking man.
   **B.** Lemon Brown was old and shabbily dressed, but Greg recognized him and
      was not afraid of him.
   **C.** The Salvation Army had helped Lemon Brown.
   **D.** Lemon Brown had crinkly white hair and whiskers.

Read the following passage. Then answer the questions that follow. Write the letter
of the correct answer on the line at the right.

> A generation has passed since Nolan Ryan threw his first major league pitch.
> His fellow players are sometimes just as eager as fans to get his autograph. Texas
> third baseman Steve Buchele, a southern California native, said, "There wasn't
> anything more exciting than coming to the games and watching Nolan pitch."
>
> How has Ryan lasted so long? He claims that it's a combination of physical
> condition and mental attitude.

[William W. Lace, *Nolan Ryan, Texas Treasure*]

**38.** Pronounce each word below, paying special attention to the final syllable. In     38. ______
   which word does the final syllable *not* rhyme with the last syllable of *generation*?
   **A.** combination          **C.** supervision
   **B.** condition            **D.** competition

**39.** Some information in the passage is important and some is not important.          39. ______
   Which information is unimportant?
   **A.** Nolan Ryan was a pitcher in the major leagues.
   **B.** Ryan was as popular with his fellow players as he was with the fans.
   **C.** Steve Buchele was a southern California native.
   **D.** Ryan has lasted so long because of a combination of physical condition and
      mental attitude.

**40.** What generalization can you form from the passage?          40. ______
   **A.** Steve Buchele played third base for Texas.
   **B.** A generation has passed since Ryan threw his first major league pitch.
   **C.** Nolan Ryan was an outstanding baseball player.
   **D.** Physical condition is more important than mental attitude in baseball.

# DECODING: TRICKY LETTER COMBINATIONS

## Introduction

When you come across unfamiliar words in your reading, try pronouncing the words. Think about the way each sound is spelled. Notice any unusual spellings. You may find that some of the words, do not sound the way they are spelled.

Note the difference between the spelling and pronunciation of the word *taught*. The letters *g* and *h* are silent. Think about other words you know that are similar in spelling to *taught*.

Suppose a passage that you are reading contains the word *haughty*. You can use what you know about the *augh* letter combination in other words to figure out how to pronounce *haughty*, which means "proud."

In words with the letter combinations *igh* and *ought, gh* is also silent, as it is in the *augh* combination. Study the examples below. (Notice that the vowel sounds in words with the *ought* combination sometimes differ.)

| Words with the *igh* combination | Words with the *ought* combination |
| --- | --- |
| fight | sought |
| right | drought |
| high | brought |

Now consider the difference between the spelling and pronunciation of the word *could*. In the *ould* combination, the *l* is silent. Think about other words you know that are similar in spelling to *could*.

**Reading Tip**
Many English words do not sound the way they are spelled. Use what you already know about words with tricky letter combinations to help you figure out the pronunciations of words that have similar combinations.

**NAME** _______________________________________________   **DATE** ___________

# Practice

Read the following passage from "Rattlesnake Hunt" by Marjorie Kinnan Rawlings.

> I hope never in my life to be so frightened as I was in those first few hours. I kept on Ross' footsteps, I moved when he moved, sometimes jolting into him when I thought he might leave me behind. He does not use the forked stick of conventional snake hunting, but a steel prong, shaped like an L, at the end of a long stout stick. He hunted casually, calling my attention to the varying vegetation, to hawks overhead, to a pair of the rare whooping cranes that flapped over us. In mid-morning he stopped short, dropped his stick, and brought up a five-foot rattlesnake draped limply over the steel L. It seemed to me that I should drop in my tracks.

**A.** Identify words in the passage that have the letter combinations shown below. Write the words below each heading. Say each word aloud. Then write its meaning next to it. If necessary, look it up in the dictionary.

| *augh* | *igh* | *ought* | *ould* |
|---|---|---|---|
|  |  |  |  |
|  |  |  |  |
|  |  |  |  |
|  |  |  |  |
|  |  |  |  |
|  |  |  |  |
|  |  |  |  |

**B. Challenge!**

In the *ough* combination at the end of words, the *gh* can be silent, or it can have the /f/ sound. Write at least one example of each case below.

**1.** *ough,* in which *gh* is silent _________________________________________

**2.** *ough,* in which *gh* has the /f/ sound _________________________________

# DECODING: SOUND/LETTER PATTERNS

## Introduction

As you explore meaning and pronunciation in your reading, you may have noticed that certain letter patterns produce specific sounds. For example, in the *tion* pattern at the end of a word, *ti* has the sound /sh/, as in *fiction* and *direction*.

Words that end with the /shən/ sound are usually spelled with the *-tion* ending. In some cases, this sound can be spelled *-sion,* as in *tension* and *expulsion,* usually when a consonant comes before the /shən/ ending.

Most words that end in a vowel plus *sion* have the /zhən/ sound, as in *decision* and *vision.*

You may have also noticed in your reading that words with more than one syllable whose last, unaccented syllable ends in *-ar, -er,* or *-or* have the same ending sound, /ər/. Examples are *dollar, deliver,* and *monitor.* The /ər/ sound does not change when *-s, -ed,* and *-ing* are added to a base word that ends in *-ar, -er,* and *-or,* as in *dollars, delivered,* and *monitoring.*

Another pattern you may have noticed is the /f/ sound produced by *ph* in words you read. The sound /f/ can be produced by the letter pattern *ph* at the beginning, in the middle, and at the end of words. Note the examples below.

- /f/ sound made by *ph* pattern at the beginning of a word: photograph, phrase, physician
- /f/ sound made by *ph* pattern in the middle of a word: gopher, emphasize, telephone
- /f/ sound made by *ph* pattern at the end of a word: graph, hieroglyph

### Reading Tip

When you discover an unfamiliar word in your reading, first try pronouncing the word. Think about the way each sound is spelled. Look for sound/letter patterns that you are familiar with, such as *tion/sion, ar/er/or,* and *ph.* Apply what you already know about sound/letter patterns to the new word. Once you are able to pronounce the word, you may discover that you are familiar with it—even though it may have seemed unfamiliar when you first saw it.

## Practice

Read the following passage from "Zoo" by Edward D. Hoch.

> This year, as the great round ship settled slowly to earth in the huge tri-city parking area just outside of Chicago, they watched with awe as the sides slowly slid up to reveal the familiar barred cages. In them were some wild breed of nightmare—small, horse-like animals that moved with quick, jerking motions and constantly chattered in a high-pitched tongue….
>
> And the crowds slowly filed by, at once horrified and fascinated by these strange creatures that looked like horses but ran up the walls of their cages like spiders. "This is certainly worth a dollar," one man remarked, hurrying away. "Im going home to get the wife."
>
> All day long it went like that, until ten thousand people had filed by the barred cages set into the side of the spaceship. Then, as the six-hour limit ran out, Professor Hugo once more took the microphone in hand. "We must go now, but we will return next year on this date. And if you enjoyed our zoo this year, telephone your friends in other cities about it. We will land in New York tomorrow, and next week on to London, Paris, Rome, Hong Kong, and Tokyo. Then on to other worlds!"

Identify words in the passage that have the sound/letter patterns shown below. Write the words below each heading.

| Words that end with *sion/tion* (can include *s* ending) | Words that have *ar/er/or* as the second, unaccented syllable (can include *s*, *ed*, and *ing* endings) | Words in which *ph* stands for the /f/ sound |
|---|---|---|
|  |  |  |
|  |  |  |
|  |  |  |
|  |  |  |
|  |  |  |
|  |  |  |

Pronounce each word aloud. Which of these words do you use in your everyday speech? What is the meaning of these words?

# DECODING: SYLLABIFICATION

## Introduction

A **syllable** is a unit of language: It can be a word or part of a word. Each syllable in a word has one vowel sound. As you explore word pronunciation and meaning during your reading, it is sometimes helpful to divide a word into its syllables.

Often, one or more of the syllables is an important clue to meaning. In addition, when you say the word aloud, you may realize that it's one you already use in your everyday speech—and you may not have recognized it by just seeing it on the page. To divide a word into syllables, first listen for the vowel sounds.

Pronounce the words *beat* and *create*. Notice that in *beat,* the letters *e* and *a* together have one vowel sound and one syllable. In *create*, the letters *e* and *a* make two different vowel sounds. *Create* has two syllables: cre ate.

Use these rules to help you divide words into syllables:

1. If a word has two vowel sounds between two consonant letters, divide the word between the two vowels.

   | | |
   |---|---|
   | ruin | ru in |
   | trial | tri al |
   | react | re act |

2. If a word has two consonants between two vowels, divide the word between the two consonants.

   | | |
   |---|---|
   | injure | in jure |
   | letter | let ter |
   | import | im port |

3. If a word has two of the same consonants next to each other, divide the word between the two consonants.

   | | |
   |---|---|
   | common | com mon |
   | effect | ef fect |
   | approve | ap prove |

4. If a word has a middle consonant between two vowels, listen for the accented syllable in the word. The middle consonant is part of the accented syllable.

   | | |
   |---|---|
   | pretend | pre tend´ |
   | melon | mel´ on |
   | salute | sa lute´ |

**Reading Tip**
Remember to listen for the vowel sounds when you divide a word into syllables.

# Practice

Read the following passage from "Two Kinds" by Amy Tan.

> Over the next year, I practiced like this, dutifully in my own way. And then one day I heard my mother and her friend Lindo Jong both talking in a loud bragging tone of voice so others could hear. It was after church, and I was leaning against the brick wall wearing a dress with stiff white petticoats. Auntie Lindo's daughter, Waverly, who was about my age, was standing farther down the wall about five feet away.

**A.** List ten words from the passage that have two syllables. (Do not list proper nouns—words that begin with capital letters.) Say each word aloud to decide how many syllables it has. Draw a line between the syllables of each word.

______________________________        ______________________________

______________________________        ______________________________

______________________________        ______________________________

______________________________        ______________________________

______________________________        ______________________________

**B.** With a partner, go through one or two of the selections in your literature book to find at least two more examples of words following each of the rules on the previous page. Then, think of words you both use in your everyday speech, and come up with at least one more example for each of the rules. Next, look through your list and circle any syllables that can stand by themselves as words. Finally, look up the meaning of each of these syllables. Explain how the syllable contributes to the overall meaning of the word.

# RECOGNIZING WORD ROOTS

## Introduction

In the English language, many words have a "core" section, or root. Consider, for example, the word *prediction*. *Pre-* and *-tion* attach to the root, *-dic-*, which means "say" in Latin. A prediction is something "said before" an event happens.

Some common roots include *dark* in *darkness*, *sad* in *sadness*, and *ground* in *foreground*. You might say that roots are the building blocks of our language. Roots are an important reading and vocabulary tool, because they can help you figure out the meaning of words that are unfamiliar.

Read the passage below from "King Arthur: The Marvel of the Sword" by Mary MacLeod.

> Then Uther Pendragon turned and said in hearing of them all: "I give my son Arthur God's blessing and mine, and bid him pray for my soul, and righteously and honorably claim the crown, on forfeiture of my blessing."
>
> And with that, King Uther died.
>
> But Arthur was still only a baby, not two years old, and Merlin knew it would be no use yet to proclaim him King. For there were many powerful nobles in England in those days, who were all trying to get the kingdom for themselves, and perhaps they would kill the little Prince. So there was much strife and debate in the land for a long time.

There are several roots in the above passage. For example, notice the word *proclaim*. If you are not familiar with a word like *proclaim* in your reading, see if the word contains a root. In this case, the root of *proclaim* is *claim*, which means "to assert." When you see that root together with the prefix *pro-*, which means "forward" or "before," you can infer that the word *proclaim* means "to assert in front of the people," or "to announce officially."

On the chart below, you will see how three words from the passage—*proclaim, righteously,* and *honorably*— are formed from root words. Notice that *righteously* is formed from the root *right* plus two suffixes: *-(e)ous*, meaning "full of," and *-ly* meaning "in the manner of." In the same way, *honorably* is formed from the root *honor* plus the suffix *-able*, which means "having qualities of," and the suffix *-ly*.

| Word | Root of Word | Meaning of Root | Meaning of Word |
|---|---|---|---|
| proclaim | claim | to assert | to announce publicly |
| righteously | right | just, lawful | in a morally just way |
| honorably | honor | reputation for goodness and justice | in a worthy, upright way |

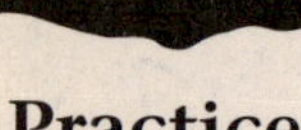




# Practice

Below, you'll find a passage from "Rip Van Winkle" by Washington Irving.
   Read the passage. As you read, look for words in the passage that have
been formed from the roots listed in the chart below. Write these larger
words in the first column of the chart. Then write the meaning of the
root, and think about how knowing the root's meaning can help you
understand the meaning of the larger word. Write the meaning of the
word in the last column of the chart.

> There was, as usual, a crowd of folk about the door, but none that Rip
> recollected. The very character of the people seemed changed. There was
> a busy, bustling, disputatious tone about it, instead of the accustomed
> drowsy tranquillity. He looked in vain for the sage Nicholas Vedder, with
> his broad face, double chin, and fair long pipe, uttering clouds of tobacco
> smoke instead of idle speeches; or Van Bummel, the schoolmaster, doling
> forth the contents of an ancient newspaper. In place of these, a lean,
> bilious-looking[37] fellow, with his pockets full of handbills, was speaking
> vehemently about rights of citizens....

37. **bilious-looking:** Looking cross or bad-tempered.

| | Word | Root of Word | Meaning of Root | Meaning of Word |
|---|---|---|---|---|
| 1. | | collect | | |
| 2. | | bustle | | |
| 3. | | dispute | | |
| 4. | | custom | | |
| 5. | | tranquil | | |
| 6. | | utter | | |
| 7. | | school | | |
| 8. | | paper | | |
| 9. | | hand | | |
| 10. | | vehement | | |

**NAME** _________________________________     **DATE** __________

# PREFIXES/SUFFIXES

## Introduction

A **prefix** is a letter or letters attached to the front of a word or root to create a new word (for example, *dis*own, *pre*text, *be*little). A **suffix** is a letter or letters attached to the end of a word or root to create a new word (for example, help*ful,* manage*able*).

By adding prefixes and suffixes to existing words, you can vastly expand your vocabulary. Learning the meanings of prefixes and suffixes will also help you to piece together the meanings of some unfamiliar words.

While you are reading, you can often figure out a word you don't know by breaking it down into its parts. For example, suppose you come across the word *inability* in your reading. You can decode the word by breaking it down into three parts (*in-abili-ty*):

1. *in-*, a prefix meaning "not" or "the opposite of"
2. *-abili-,* from *able,* a word meaning "having enough power or skill to do something"
3. *-ty,* a suffix meaning "a condition or quality"

When you look at the word parts, you realize that *inability* means "the condition of not having enough power or skill to do something."

The chart below lists several common prefixes and suffixes and explains what they mean. Study the chart so you can recall these meanings when you are reading a textbook or story. Knowledge of prefixes and suffixes will save you a lot of time when you are trying to decode words as you read.

| Prefix | Meaning | Suffix | Meaning |
|---|---|---|---|
| *be-* | completely, excessively | *-er* | one that performs a certain task |
| *circum-* | around, about | *-est* | the most; forms the superlative degree |
| *dis-* | not | *-graph* | something written or drawn |
| *in-* | not, in, into, within | *-ly* | in the manner of |
| *pre-* | before, prior to | *-ment* | action, process |
| *un-* | opposite of | *-ness* | state, quality, degree |
| *re-* | again, anew | *-ology* | science, study |
| *non-* | not | *-ty* | condition, quality |

     Prefixes/Suffixes   **19**

## Practice

As you read the passage below from "How to Enjoy Poetry" by James Dickey, suppose that you don't know the meanings of the words *re-created, possibilities,* and *unexpectedness.* These words are listed on the chart below the passage. On the chart, write any prefix or suffix contained in these words and what the prefix or suffix means. Then figure out the meaning of each word, and write that meaning in the last column of the chart.

The more your encounter with poetry deepens, the more your experience of your own life will deepen, and you will begin to see things by means of words, and words by means of things.

You will come to understand the world as it interacts with words, as it can be re-created by words, by rhythms and by images.

You'll understand that this condition is one charged with vital possibilities. You will pick up meaning more quickly—and you will *create* meaning, too, for yourself and for others.

Connections between things will exist for you in ways that they never did before. They will shine with unexpectedness, wide-openness, and you will go toward them, on your own path.

| Word | Prefix | Suffix | Root | Meaning |
|------|--------|--------|------|---------|
| 1. re-created | | | create | |
| 2. possibilities | | | possible | |
| 3. unexpected-ness | | | expect | |

# INFLECTED FORMS: PLURALS AND TENSES

## Introduction

An **inflection** is a sound that is added to the end of a word. It changes the word's meaning in some way. Compare the two words *tax* and *taxes*. The sound /iz/ has been added to the stem word *tax*, and it changes the meaning from singular to plural. "Beaches" is what is called an **inflected form.** The *-es* is the inflection, a special kind of suffix. In English, the sound of the inflections *-s, -es,* or *-es* is used to change many singular nouns to plural nouns.

Inflections are also used to change the tense of verbs. For example, *enter* and *entered*. Notice how the addition of the sound /ed/ changes this verb from the present to the past tense.

There are other uses of inflections in English, but these are two of the most important. Understanding how inflections are used will increase your understanding of grammar and help you be a better writer.

Read the passage below from "After Twenty Years" by O. Henry.

> The man from the West unfolded the little piece of paper handed him. His hand was steady when he began to read, but it trembled a little by the time he had finished. The note was rather short.

The stems of the inflected verbs are *unfold, hand, tremble*, and *finish*. The inflected forms let you know that the action takes place in the past. The narrator is telling the reader about it. Inflections are also important in subject-verb agreement. For example, in the present tense you would say "the man unfolds the paper," not "the man unfolded the paper." Notice that the *-s* inflection is used here. This is the same sound used to change many singular nouns to plurals.

## Practice

Read the passage below from "Justin Lebo" by Phillip Hoose. Watch for both plural and tense inflections. (*Hint:* Watch for plural nouns and for verbs in the past tense.)

> Each time he told his story, Justin asked for bikes and money. "The first few interviews were fun," Justin says, "but it reached a point where I really didn't like doing them. The publicity was necessary, though. I had to keep doing interviews to get the donations I needed."
>
> By the time school opened, he was working on ten bikes at a time. There were so many calls now that he was beginning to refuse offers that weren't the exact bikes he needed.
>
> As checks came pouring in, Justin's money problems disappeared. He set up a bank account and began to make bulk orders of common parts from Mel's bike shop. Mel seemed delighted to see him. Sometimes, if Justin brought a bike by the shop, Mel would help him fix it. When Justin tried to talk him into a lower price for big orders, Mel smiled and gave in. He respected another good businessman. They became friends.

**A.** List two inflected nouns from the passage above. How does the inflection change their meaning?

_______________________________________________________________

_______________________________________________________________

**B.** List five inflected verbs from the passage above. List those with /ed/ sound endings in one list and those with /t/ sound endings in another. How do the inflections change the meaning of the verbs?

_______________________________________________________________

_______________________________________________________________

# CONTEXT CLUES

## Introduction

When you read an unfamiliar word, you can use **context clues** to figure out its meaning. Context clues are clues in the text surrounding a word. Look for context clues in the sentence that contains the unfamiliar word or in the phrases or sentences nearby.

### Model 1

The following passage is from "A Boy and a Man" by James Ramsey Ullman. Notice how the underlined parts of the sentence might help readers to define the word *pummeled*.

> Pulling the boy to his feet, he helped him dress. Then he rubbed and **pummeled** him until at last Rudi felt the warmth of returning circulation.

| Unfamiliar Word | Context Clues | Definition |
| --- | --- | --- |
| pummeled | rubbed; felt the warmth of returning circulation | beat or hit again and again |

### Model 2

In the passage from "The Third Wish" below, Joan Aiken uses the word *extricate*. Study the underlined phrases to find context clues that help you define this word. As you read the passage, create a definition for the word *extricate* in your mind. Then compare your definition with the one in the chart below.

> Mr. Peters ran down the hill and as he neared the bushes he saw something white among them which was trying to **extricate** itself; coming closer he found that it was a swan that had become entangled in the thorns growing on the bank of the canal.

| Unfamiliar Word | Context Clues | Definition |
| --- | --- | --- |
| extricate | trying; entangled in the thorns | set free, release |

# Practice

## Part I

Read the passage below from "The Princess and the Tin Box" by James Thurber. Then complete the chart.

> Now the fifth prince was the strongest and handsomest of all the five suitors, but he was the son of a poor king whose realm had been overrun by mice and locusts and wizards and mining engineers so that there was nothing much of value left in it. He came plodding up to the palace of the princess on a plow horse and he brought her a small tin box filled with mica and feldspar and hornblende[3] which he had picked up on the way.
>
> The other princes roared with disdainful laughter when they saw the tawdry gift the fifth prince had brought to the princess. But she examined it with great interest and squealed with delight, for all her life she had been glutted with precious stones and priceless metals, but she had never seen tin before or mica or feldspar or hornblende.

3. **mica, feldspar, hornblende:** Common minerals found in rocks.

| Unfamiliar Word | Context Clues | Definition |
|---|---|---|
| disdainful | | |
| tawdry | | |
| glutted | | |

## Part II

The following passage is from "Two Kinds" by Amy Tan. As you read the passage, circle the context clues that might help you define the underlined words. Then complete the chart on the next page.

> But my mother's expression was what devastated me: a quiet, blank look that said she had lost everything. I felt the same way, and it seemed as if everybody were now coming up, like gawkers at the scene of an accident, to see what parts were actually missing. When we got on the bus to go home, my father was humming the busy-bee tune and my mother was silent. I kept thinking she wanted to wait until we got home before shouting at me. But when my father unlocked the door to our apartment, my mother walked in and then went to the back, into the bedroom. No accusations. No blame. And in a way, I felt disappointed. I had been waiting for her to start shouting, so I could shout back and cry and blame her for all my misery.
>
> I assumed my talent-show fiasco meant I never had to play the piano again. But two days later, after school, my mother came out of the kitchen and saw me watching TV.
>
> "Four clock," she reminded me as if it were any other day. I was stunned, as though she were asking me to go through the talent-show torture again. I wedged myself more tightly in front of the TV.

NAME _______________________________ DATE __________

## Part II (continued)

| Unfamiliar Word | Context Clues | Definition |
|---|---|---|
| devastated | | |
| gawkers | | |
| accusations | | |
| fiasco | | |

NAME _________________________________     DATE __________

# ACTIVE READING: SET A PURPOSE

## Introduction

Different types of writing present different reasons for reading. For example, we read textbooks for a different reason than we might read magazines. When reading a textbook, you might skim for information to prepare for a test. When reading a magazine, you might read quickly for entertainment. Before sitting down to read, you might want to set a purpose for reading.

Setting a purpose for reading involves identifying specific questions that you will answer during reading. By asking yourself specific questions before you begin, you direct your attention to the key ideas in the passage. You can get an idea of what the selection is about by looking at the:

- title
- subheadings
- illustrations

You might also want to read the first sentence or passage for further information. Use three steps to help you set a purpose:

1. Study the title and illustrations.
2. Read the first sentence or paragraph.
3. Look for clues in the text. (Is the writing informative or entertaining?)

### Model

Read the following beginning of an essay called "All Together Now" by Barbara Jordan. Think of your own questions that you could use to set a purpose for reading this selection. Then compare your questions to the ones below.

> When I look at race relations today I can see that some positive changes have come about. But much remains to be done, and the answer does not lie in more legislation. We *have* the legislation we need; we have the laws. Frankly, I don't believe that the task of bringing us all together can be accomplished by government. What we need now is soul force—the efforts of people working on a small scale to build a truly tolerant, harmonious society. And parents can do a great deal to create that tolerant society.

### Questions

Why would you read this passage? What information might you expect to find?

### Purpose for Reading

- To find out more about what the writer means by "soul force."
- To find out what parents can do to create a better, more tolerant society.

## Practice

Below is another passage from "All Together Now" by Barbara Jordan.
Read the passage, and then answer the questions below.

> What can parents do? We can put our faith in young people as a positive force. I have yet to find a racist baby. Babies come into the world as blank as slates and, with their beautiful innocence, see others not as different but as enjoyable companions. Children learn ideas and attitudes from the adults who nurture them. I absolutely believe that children do not adopt prejudices unless they absorb them from their parents or teachers.
>
> The best way to get this country faithful to the American dream of tolerance and equality is to start small. Parents can actively encourage their children to be in the company of people who are of other racial and ethnic backgrounds. If a child thinks, "Well, that person's color is not the same as mine, but she must be okay because she likes to play with the same things I like to play with," that child will grow up with a broader view of humanity.

Answer the following questions.

1. What do you think might be the purpose or purposes for reading the passage? Why?

   _______________________________________________________________

   _______________________________________________________________

2. List at least three details you learned about prejudice and tolerance from reading this passage.

   a. ___________________________________________________________

   b. ___________________________________________________________

   c. ___________________________________________________________

## B. Challenge!

List three different kinds of books or written texts you might read on your own and your purpose for reading them.

| | Type of Book or Text | Purpose for Reading |
|---|---|---|
| 1. | | |
| 2. | | |
| 3. | | |

# ACTIVE READING: PREDICT

## Introduction

When you use what you *know* to explain what you *think* is going to happen, you are making a **prediction.** Predictions are based on two factors:

- information from the story
- knowledge from your own personal experience

Making predictions can make reading more exciting because you become actively involved with what you are reading.

**Making Predictions: Three Steps**

### Step 1

Ask yourself what you know about the story and the characters so far; look for descriptions and clues in the text and make notes to yourself about those clues and details.

### Step 2

Ask yourself what your own personal experiences have taught you about the details you wrote in your notes.

### Step 3

Based on what you discovered in steps 1 and 2, ask yourself what you think will happen. Write your predictions down on a piece of paper.

**Reading Tip**

To help you make predictions in your reading, think about other stories and books you have read.

- What predictions did you make?
- Was the story different from your expectations? If so, how?
- What surprised you about the story if anything?
- Were your predictions correct?

## Practice

Suppose that you were about to read an ancient Greek myth entitled
"Icarus and Daedalus." Answer the following question.

1. What would the title lead you to expect about the story?

_______________________________________________________________

Read this passage from "Icarus and Daedalus," and answer the questions.

Daedalus managed to escape from his cell; but it seemed impossible to
leave the island, since every ship that came or went was well guarded by
order of the king.

At length, watching the sea-gulls in the air…he thought of a plan for
himself and his young son Icarus, who was captive with him.

Little by little, he gathered a store of feathers great and small. He fastened
these together with thread, molded them in with wax, and so fashioned
two great wings like those of a bird. When they were done, Daedalus fitted
them to his own shoulders, and…learned to fly.

Without delay, he fell to work on a pair of wings for the boy Icarus,
and taught him carefully how to use them, bidding him beware of rash
adventures among the stars. "Remember…never to fly very low or very
high, for the fogs about the earth would weigh you down, but the blaze
of the sun will surely melt your feathers apart if you go too near."

2. What do you think will happen in the next few paragraphs of the myth?

_______________________________________________________________

3. What details in the passage helped you make this prediction?

_______________________________________________________________

Now read the rest of the passage and answer the questions.

But when a great wind filled their wings, and Icarus felt himself sustained,
…he forgot everything in the world but joy. He…saw but vaguely that
wingèd thing in the distance…that was his father Daedalus. He longed
for one draft of flight to quench the thirst of his captivity; he stretched
out his arms to the sky and made towards the highest heavens.

…Warmer and warmer grew the air. Those arms, that had seemed to
uphold him, relaxed. His wings wavered, drooped. He fluttered his young
hands vainly—he was falling—and in that terror he remembered. The heat
of the sun had melted the wax from his wings;…there was none to help.

4. How were your predictions like the actual events of the story?

_______________________________________________________________

5. How were your predictions different from the events in the story?

_______________________________________________________________

                    

**NAME** _______________________________________________  **DATE** _____________

# ACTIVE READING: QUESTION AND CLARIFY

## Introduction

*Question:* Asking yourself questions as you read can help improve your reading comprehension. The first step is identifying what is confusing to you.
*Clarify:* Often, the answer to your question can be found in the text, either at an earlier point or later. When you have a question while reading:

- Stop to think.
- Look back over the material you have already read to try to find clues to the answer.
- Continue reading, keeping your question in mind. Often you'll discover the answer later in the text.

### Model

Read the passage below from "A Boy and a Man" by James Ramsey Ullman. Note the interrupter questions in italics.

The crevasse[1] was about six feet wide at the top and narrowed gradually as it went down. But how deep it was Rudi could not tell.

*Where are these events taking place? Who is Rudi, and what is he doing? What is a crevasse?*

After a few feet the blue walls of ice curved away at a sharp slant, and what was below the curve was hidden from sight.

*I see: the footnote says that a "crevasse" is a deep crack in a glacier. The action must be taking place somewhere in the mountains. Rudi seems to be looking down into the crevasse.*

"Hello!" Rudi called.
"Hello—" A voice answered from the depths.

*Has someone fallen into the crevasse? I'll probably learn more as I read.*

"How far down are you?"
"I'm not sure. About twenty feet, I'd guess."
"On the bottom?"
"No. I can't even see the bottom. I was lucky and hit a ledge."
The voice spoke in German, but with a strange accent. Whoever was down there, Rudi knew, it was not one of the men of the valley.
"Are you hurt?" he called.
"Nothing broken—no," said the voice. "Just shaken up some. And cold."

*I was right. Someone did fall into the crevasse and can't get out. Since the language is German, the action may be taking place in Europe.*

## Practice

Below is a passage from "Nosing Around U.S. Borders" by Susan Essoyan. As you read the passage below, ask yourself questions about what is happening.

> The well-dressed tourist took her eyes off the baggage carousel for a moment, smiled and cooed in Japanese, "Hello, little Mr. Woof-Woof. Here you are."
>
> She plopped her bag on the ground for the veteran detective, a beagle called Junior, who trotted forward to get a whiff. When the dog finished and turned away, signaling that the bag had passed inspection, the woman dissolved into laughter.
>
> "They think he's cute," said Junior's handler, Mike Simon, the U.S. Department of Agriculture's (USDA) senior canine officer in Honolulu. Travelers don't object to Junior's search, which is not always the case with traditional inspections. "He's more like a mascot," Simon said.
>
> Despite Junior's engaging personality, the 6-year-old dog has a serious mission: to help protect U.S. agriculture from foreign pests and diseases. He and the 60 other dogs in the USDA's Beagle Brigade cruise international airports across the country in search of forbidden fruit, vegetables, plants and meat.

1. While you were reading the passage, what questions did you have?

_______________________________________________

_______________________________________________

_______________________________________________

2. What information in the passage helped clarify the answers to these questions?

_______________________________________________

_______________________________________________

_______________________________________________

_______________________________________________

     

# ACTIVE READING: CONNECT

## Introduction

There are many ways to respond to something that you are reading. One of the most natural responses is to think how the literature relates to your own experiences or to another text that you have read. As you read, you may **connect** to a character or to something that character says or does. Sometimes, you will be reminded of another story you once read or something that you recently learned. Making connections as you read allows you to relate to the text in your own personal way.

To make connections in your reading, ask yourself questions such as those below. They will help you to become a more active reader by giving you ideas about how you can connect to what you are reading.

**Questions to Help You Connect**

- How do I relate to this character?
- Am I like this person? Do I know someone like this person?
- Would I have done or said the same thing as this person?
- Is there anything in this story that is similar to my life, my own experiences, or the experiences of someone that I know?
- In what ways is this story like another story that I have read?

*Model*

The passage below, from "The Hummingbird That Lived Through Winter" by William Saroyan, tells about how a boy and his neighbor, an old man named Dikran, once tried to save a tiny bird. As you read the passage, connect it to your own experiences, ideas, or perhaps another story you have read. The connections you make may be similar to or different from some of the sample connections shown below.

> There was a hummingbird once which in the wintertime did not leave our neighborhood in Fresno, California.
>
> I'll tell you about it.
>
> Across the street lived old Dikran, who was almost blind. He was past eighty and his wife was only a few years younger. They had a little house that was as neat inside as it was ordinary outside—except for old Dikran's garden, which was the best thing of its kind in the world. Plants, bushes, trees—all strong, in sweet black moist earth whose guardian was old Dikran. All things from the sky loved this spot in our poor neighborhood, and old Dikran loved *them*.

**Possible Connections**

- I once saw a picture of a hummingbird.
- Dikran and his wife are as old as my grandparents are.
- The garden reminds me of a place in our neighborhood.
- My older sister loves gardening, too.

NAME __________________________  DATE __________

## Practice

Below is a passage from "Justin Lebo" by Phillip Hoose. As you read the selection, think about how you connect to it and respond by writing your ideas in the appropriate sections below.

> It was a BMX bike with a twenty-inch frame. Its original color was buried beneath five or six coats of gunky paint. Now it showed up as sort of a rusted red. Everything—the grips, the pedals, the brakes, the seat, the spokes—was bent or broken, twisted and rusted. Justin stood back as if he were inspecting a painting for sale at an auction. Then he made his final judgment: perfect.
>
> Justin talked the owner down to $6.50 and asked his mother, Diane, to help him load the bike into the back of their car.
>
> When he got it home, he wheeled the junker into the garage and showed it proudly to his father. "Will you help me fix it up?" he asked. Justin's hobby was bike racing, a passion the two of them shared. Their garage barely had room for the car anymore. It was more like a bike shop. Tires and frames hung from hooks on the ceiling, and bike wrenches dangled from the walls.

1. Do you know anyone whom one or more of the characters in the passage call to mind?

   ______________________________________________

   ______________________________________________

2. Do any of the descriptions or events in the passage remind you of experiences in your own life? Explain.

   ______________________________________________

   ______________________________________________

   ______________________________________________

3. Do you connect with any of the feelings the characters have?

   ______________________________________________

   ______________________________________________

   ______________________________________________

4. Does this passage remind you of another story? In what way?

   ______________________________________________

   ______________________________________________

   ______________________________________________

# ACTIVE READING: SQ3R

## Introduction

Most of the time, people read for either pleasure or to learn about new things. When "reading to learn," it is helpful to use the **SQ3R** strategy. This strategy helps you understand and remember what you read, especially when you are reading a difficult or unfamiliar text.

SQ3R stands for the five steps a reader can use to remember information.

| | |
|---|---|
| **Survey** | Survey the text and get a general idea of what it is about. Read the first sentence of each paragraph. |
| **Question** | Keep in mind questions you have as you look over the selection. What do you want to find out in the selection? What looks unclear to you? |
| **Read** | Read the text carefully from the beginning. Pause to think about what you are reading and to make sure you understand it. Look up unknown words and reread difficult sentences or paragraphs. |
| **Recite** | See how well you understood and remember the text by reciting what you learned out loud. Recite the information to yourself or to a friend. **Helpful Hint:** Try to answer these questions: Who? What? Where? When? Why? How? |
| **Review** | Summarize the text and think about the main ideas by talking with someone else about it. You may also want to make an outline, use note cards, or make an illustration to help you remember key points. |

# Practice

Practice using the SQ3R strategy with the passage below. Do not read the entire passage first. Follow the steps below.

**I. Survey**

What does this passage seem to be about?

_______________________________________________________________

**II. Question**

Write some questions that you have.

_______________________________________________________________

_______________________________________________________________

**III. Read**

Read the passage from "Tenochtitlan: Inside the Aztec Capital" by Jacqueline Dineen. Pause as you read to make sure that you understand it.

> **Inside the City** The Spaniards' first view of Tenochtitlan was described by one of Cortés's[6] soldiers, Bernal Diaz: "And when we saw all those towns and level causeways leading into Mexico, we were astounded. These great towns and buildings rising from the water, all made of stone, seemed like an enchanted vision."
>
> By that time Tenochtitlan was the largest city in Mexico. About 200,000 people lived there. The houses were one story high and had flat roofs. In the center of the city was a large square. The twin temple stood on one side, and the king's palace on another. Officials' houses made of white stone also lined the square. There were few roads. People traveled in canoes along canals.

6. **Hernando Cortés:** Spanish adventurer (1485–1547) who conquered what is now central and southern Mexico.

**IV. Recite**

Verbalize what you have just read by telling yourself or a friend about it.

**V. Review**

In your notebook, write a brief summary or outline of the passage.

     

**NAME** _______________________________________________ **DATE** ____________

# IDENTIFY MAIN IDEAS AND SUPPORTING DETAILS

## Introduction

The **main idea** of a passage is its central and most important idea. Effective readers look for this central idea as they read. The main idea can appear at the beginning, middle, or end of a passage.

Writers reinforce their main ideas with **supporting details.** These words, phrases, or sentences tell something about the main idea. They can be facts, statistics, dates, names, opinions, or details.

The main idea of a passage can be stated clearly in one sentence in the selection. This is called a **stated main idea.** Sometimes the main idea is not stated in any one sentence but is a summary of the information in the passage. This is called an **implied main idea.** When you are reading, begin to identify the main idea, whether stated or implied, and look for its supporting details.

### Model 1

In the following example from "The Iceman" by Don Lessem, the under-lined sentence is the stated main idea. Each sentence that follows provides support for the idea.

> Ötzi was a welcome visitor to the villages along his route. If he was a shepherd, he would have brought the villagers meat (since wool was not yet used for clothing). If he was a trader, he would have brought them flint for tools or copper for weapons.

### Model 2

In this example from "The Lion and the Statue" by Aesop, the main idea is implied rather than stated directly.

> A Man and a Lion were discussing the relative[1] strength of men and lions in general. The Man contended[2] that he and his fellows were stronger than lions by reason of their greater intelligence.
>
> "Come now with me," he cried, "and I will soon prove that I am right." So he took him into the public gardens and showed him a statue of Hercules[3] overcoming the Lion and tearing his mouth in two.
>
> "That is all very well," said the Lion, "but proves nothing, for it was a man who made the statue."

1. **relative:** Comparative.
2. **contended:** Argued.
3. **Hercules:** Hero of ancient Greek mythology known for his strength.

The implied main idea might be stated as follows: What we think is true depends on our perspective, or point of view.

NAME _______________________________     DATE _______________

# Practice

### Part I

Below is a passage from "Melting Pot" by Anna Quindlen. Read the
passage and answer the questions that follow.

> Yet somehow now we seem to have reached a nice mix. About a third of
> the people in the neighborhood think of squid as calamari, about a third
> think of it as sushi, and about a third think of it as bait. Lots of the single
> people who have moved in during the last year or two are easy-going
> and good-tempered about all the kids. The old Italians have become
> philosophical about the new Hispanics, although they still think more
> of them should know English.

1. What statement best expresses the main idea of this passage?

   _______________________________________________________

2. Is the main idea implied or stated?

   _______________________________________________________

3. Identify at least three supporting details in this passage. Write the
   details in the spaces provided.

   a. _________________________________________________

   _________________________________________________

   b. _________________________________________________

   _________________________________________________

   c. _________________________________________________

   _________________________________________________

**Part II**

Below is a passage from "The Hummingbird That Lived Through Winter"
by William Saroyan. Read the passage and answer the questions that follow.

> The transformation was incredible. The old man kept his hand gener-
> ously open, and I expected the helpless bird to shoot upward out of his
> hand, suspend itself in space, and scare the life out of me—which is
> exactly what happened. The new life of the little bird was magnificent.
> It spun about in the little kitchen, going to the window, coming back to
> the heat, suspending, circling as if it were summertime and it had never
> felt better in its whole life.

**1.** What statement best expresses the main idea of this passage?

_______________________________________________

_______________________________________________

_______________________________________________

_______________________________________________

**2.** Is the main idea implied or stated? _______________________________

**3.** Identify three supporting details in this passage. Write the details in
the spaces provided.

a. _______________________________________________

_______________________________________________

b. _______________________________________________

_______________________________________________

c. _______________________________________________

_______________________________________________

**NAME** ___________________________________________   **DATE** ______________

## Part III

Below is a passage from "Seventh Grade" by Gary Soto. Read the passage
and answer the questions that follow.

> The small, triangle-shaped campus bustled with students talking about
> their new classes. Everyone was in a sunny mood. Victor hurried to the
> bag lunch area, where he sat down and opened his math book. He moved
> his lips as if he were reading, but his mind was somewhere else. He raised
> his eyes slowly and looked around. No Teresa.
>
> He lowered his eyes, pretending to study, then looked slowly to the
> left. No Teresa. He turned a page in the book and stared at some math
> problems that scared him because he knew he would have to do them
> eventually. He looked to the right. Still no sign of her. He stretched out
> lazily in an attempt to disguise his snooping.

1. What statement best expresses the main idea of this passage?

   _________________________________________________________

   _________________________________________________________

   _________________________________________________________

   _________________________________________________________

2. Is the main idea implied or stated? _______________________

3. Identify three supporting details in this passage. Write the details in
   the spaces provided.

   a. ______________________________________________________

   ________________________________________________________

   b. ______________________________________________________

   ________________________________________________________

   c. ______________________________________________________

   ________________________________________________________

# MAKE INFERENCES

## Introduction

Writers don't always describe everything that is happening. It is up to the reader to figure out why characters may be acting or feeling a certain way. When readers draw these types of conclusions, they are **making inferences.** Your own experiences and prior knowledge will help you to make inferences, or reasonable guesses, as you read. In addition, use textual clues to draw certain conclusions. These inferences will help you to understand the selection better and to identify what the author is communicating.

Keep this equation in mind to understand how to make inferences.

Textual Clues + What You Know = Inference

### Model

Read the passage below from *The Midwife's Apprentice* by Karen Cushman. Then look at the chart to see how certain inferences were made.

> While they ate their bread-and-bacon supper, while Alyce helped Edward mound up straw in a corner of the kitchen, while she sat by watching for him to go to sleep, all the while Edward talked of life on the manor. He told her of the silken-robed lords and ladies who came for feasts and rode out to hunt and danced like autumn leaves in the candlelit great hall, of the visiting knights who clanked their swords against each other as they practiced in the school yard, of the masons who slapped mortar and bricks together to build a great new tower at the corner of the hall that looked to stretch near all the way to heaven. He described the excitement of buying and selling at the great autumn horse fair, the nervous preparations accompanying the arrival of some velvet-shod bishop or priest, and the thrill of watching the baron's men ride out to confront a huge maddened boar who had roamed too close to the village. And he complained at his lot, doing all the smallest tasks, not being allowed to help with the threshing and ploughing, being teased for being so little and frail and tied to Cook's skirts and fit for nothing but gathering eggs.

| Textual Clues | + What You Know | = Inference |
|---|---|---|
| bread-and-bacon supper | simple foods | The characters may be poor or from a humble position in society. |
| lords and ladies, candlelit great hall, knights, baron | These details fit in with what I know about the Middle Ages. | The story is probably set in medieval times. |
| Edward complained at his lot. | Young children are often eager to grow up. | Edward is restless and wants more independence. |

## Practice

Below is a passage from "All Summer in a Day" by Ray Bradbury. As you read the passage, look for clues that help you make inferences about what is happening. Then answer the questions that follow.

> They edged away from her, they would not look at her. She felt them go away. And this was because she would play no games with them in the echoing tunnels of the underground city. If they tagged her and ran, she stood blinking after them and did not follow. When the class sang songs about happiness and life and games her lips barely moved. Only when they sang about the sun and the summer did her lips move as she watched the drenched windows.
>
> And then, of course, the biggest crime of all was that she had come here only five years ago from Earth, and she remembered the sun and the way the sun was and the sky was when she was four in Ohio. And they, they had been on Venus all their lives, and they had been only two years old when last the sun came out and had long since forgotten the color and heat of it and the way it really was. But Margot remembered.

1. What inference can you make about the way Margot feels about the other children? About the way they feel about her?

   _______________________________________________________________

   _______________________________________________________________

2. What clues helped you to make these inferences?

   _______________________________________________________________

   _______________________________________________________________

3. What inference can you make about everyday life on Venus?

   _______________________________________________________________

   _______________________________________________________________

4. What clues helped you to make this inference?

   _______________________________________________________________

   _______________________________________________________________

# CLASSIFY/CATEGORIZE

## Introduction

When you **classify** or **categorize**, you arrange things into classes or groups according to a system, For example, dogs and cats are both classified as animals, but each can be further classified into different types of dogs or cats.

This chart may help clarify the relationship of the things to be classified and their division into groups.

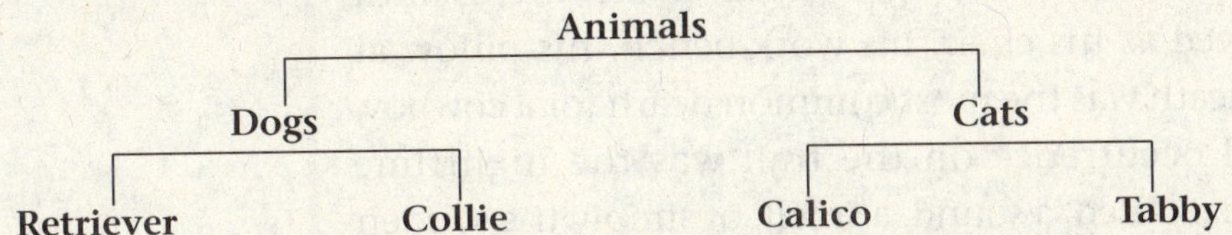


In much of your reading, you will come upon examples of classification. Classifying is a technique that writers use to organize a passage. Writers help readers understand a point they are making by classifying ideas or things into a group. While you are reading, look for examples of this technique. Notice how classifying helps you recognize similarities and differences in a subject and helps explain an idea by providing specific examples or details.

### *Model*

Read the following passage from "The Real Story of a Cowboy's Life" by Geoffrey C. Ward.

> A drive's success depended on discipline and planning. According to Teddy Blue,[1] most Texas herds numbered about 2,000 head with a trail boss and about a dozen men in charge—though herds as large as 15,000 were also driven north with far larger escorts. The most experienced men rode "point" and "swing," at the head and sides of the long herd; the least experienced brought up the rear, riding "drag" and eating dust.

1. **Teddy Blue:** Edward C. Abbot; a cowboy who rode in a successful trail drive in the 1880's.

Study the chart below to see how Geoffrey C. Ward classifies/categorizes the herds of cattle according to their size and the cowboys riding the trail according to their experience.

| Size of Herd | Categories of Cowboy |
| --- | --- |
| Most Texas herds: about 2,000 | Most experienced: rode at the head and sides of the herd |
| Some herds: up to 15,000 | Least experienced: rode at the rear |

## Practice

Below is another passage from "The Real Story of a Cowboy's Life" by
Geoffrey C. Ward. Read the passage and follow the instructions below.

> They had to learn to work as a team, keeping the herd moving during
> the day, resting peacefully at night. Twelve to fifteen miles a day was a
> good pace. But such steady progress could be interrupted at any time. A
> cowboy had to know how to gauge the temperament of his cattle, how
> to chase down a stray without alarming the rest of the herd, how to lasso[2]
> a steer using the horn of his saddle as a tying post. His saddle was his most
> prized possession; it served as his chair, his work-bench, his pillow at
> night. Being dragged to death was the most common death for a cowboy,
> and so the most feared occurrence on the trail was the nighttime
> stampede.[3] As Teddy Blue recalled, a sound, a smell, or simply the sudden
> movement of a jittery cow could set off a whole herd.

2. **lasso:** To throw a long rope with a sliding noose at one end over something, and then
   pulling the noose tight and catching it.
3. **stampede:** Sudden rush of panicked animals.

1. According to the passage, what kinds of knowledge did a cowboy
   need to have?

   _______________________________________________________

   _______________________________________________________

2. Why is a cowboy's saddle classified as his most prized possession?

   _______________________________________________________

   _______________________________________________________

3. What three causes are classified together as reasons that a herd might
   stampede?

   _______________________________________________________

   _______________________________________________________

# COMPARE AND CONTRAST

## Introduction

As you read, look for the writer's use of comparisons and contrasts. A writer uses **comparison** to show how things are similar and uses **contrast** to show how things are different. While reading, look for clue words that may help you recognize a comparison or contrast. Clue words and phrases that may signal a comparison are *like, similar to,* and *in the same way.* Words and phrases that may signal a contrast are *but, different from,* and *however.*

### Model

Read the passage below from "The Cat Who Thought She Was a Dog and the Dog Who Thought He Was a Cat" by Isaac Bashevis Singer. Look for the comparisons and contrasts and compare them to the ones below.

> The first time the cat sprang up on the bench and saw her image in the mirror, she became terribly perplexed. She had never before seen such a creature. Kot's whiskers bristled, she began to meow at her reflection and raised a paw to it, but the other creature meowed back and raised her paw too. Soon the dog jumped up on the bench, and when he saw the other dog he became wild with rage and shock. He barked at the other dog and showed him his teeth, but the other barked back and bared his fangs too. So great was the distress of Burek and Kot that for the first time in their lives they turned on each other. Burek took a bite out of Kot's throat and Kot hissed and spat at him and clawed his muzzle. They both started to bleed and the sight of blood aroused them so that they nearly killed or crippled each other. The members of the household barely managed to separate them. Because a dog is stronger than a cat, Burek had to be tied outside, and he howled all day and all night. In their anguish, both the dog and the cat stopped eating.

### Comparison

- Both the dog and the cat became angry at seeing their reflections.
- Both the dog and the cat turned on each other.
- They both stopped eating.

### Contrast

- A dog is stronger than a cat, so the dog was tied outside.

## Practice

**A.** Below is a passage from "The Night the Bed Fell" by James Thurber.
Read the passage and answer the questions below.

> …Then there was Aunt Sarah Shoaf, who never went to bed at night
> without the fear that a burglar was going to get in and blow chloroform[6]
> under her door through a tube. To avert this calamity—for she was in
> greater dread of anesthetics than of losing her household goods—she
> always piled her money, silverware, and other valuables in a neat stack
> just outside her bedroom, with a note reading: "This is all I have. Please
> take it and do not use your chloroform, as this is all I have." Aunt Gracie
> Shoaf also had a burglar phobia, but she met it with more fortitude. She
> was confident that burglars had been getting into her house every night
> for forty years. The fact that she never missed any thing was to her no
> proof to the contrary. She always claimed that she scared them off before
> they could take anything, by throwing shoes down the hallway. When
> she went to bed she piled, where she could get at them handily, all the
> shoes there were about her house.

6. **chloroform:** Substance used at one time as an anesthetic, or pain-killer, during
   operations because it can cause a person to pass out.

**1.** How was Aunt Sarah Shoaf like Aunt Gracie Shoaf?

_______________________________________________________________

_______________________________________________________________

**2.** How was Aunt Gracie different from Aunt Sarah?

_______________________________________________________________

_______________________________________________________________

**B.** Circle the clue words that help you recognize comparisons and
contrasts.
   **1.** Briggs Beall and I were in the same room, but my brother Roy
      slept in a room across the hall.
   **2.** My bed was like an army cot.
   **3.** The two sides were similar to those of a drop-leaf table.
   **4.** I told Briggs that I was a light sleeper; however, the truth is that I
      am always slow to wake up.
   **5.** My mother's reaction to the events on the night the bed fell was
      different from my father's reaction.

**C. Challenge!**
Research living conditions in another country of your choice. List
five comparisons and five contrasts to living in your country.

            

**NAME** _______________________________    **DATE** _____________

# FOLLOW A SEQUENCE OF EVENTS

## Introduction

The **sequence of events** in a passage is the chronological, or time, order of those events.

   While you read, in order to help you follow the sequence of events, you may want to make a timeline. A timeline not only enables you to follow the series of events but also to see the pattern of events that is developing. To make a timeline, draw a horizontal line. Draw a short vertical line for each important event in the sequence. At each vertical line, write a few words describing the event.

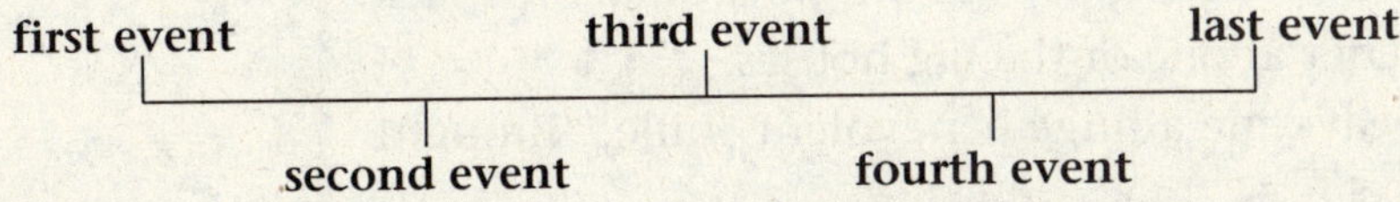


**Helpful Hint:** Look for clue words that may signal a sequence, such as *first, second, next, then, finally,* and *last.*

*Model*

Make a timeline for the events in this passage from "Amigo Brothers" by Piri Thomas. When you have finished your work, compare your timeline to the one below.

> Antonio knew the dynamite that was stored in his *amigo* brother's fist. He ducked a short right and missed a left hook. Felix trapped him against the ropes just long enough to pour some punishing rights and lefts to Antonio's hard midsection. Antonio slipped away from Felix, crashing two lefts to his head, which set Felix's right ear to ringing.
>
>   Bong! Both *amigos* froze a punch well on its way, sending up a roar of approval for good sportsmanship.

**Timeline**

1. Antonio ducks a short right.
2. Felix traps Antonio against the ropes.
3. Antonio slips away from Felix.
4. He lands two lefts to Felix's head.
5. Round ends and crowd roars.

**NAME** _________________________________________________ **DATE** _____________

# Practice

### 1. Timeline

Make a timeline for this passage from "Cat on the Go" by James Herriot. The horizontal line has already been drawn for you.

> Then one evening a man brought in a dog for a distemper[13] inoculation and left the front door open. When I went up to our flat I found that Oscar had disappeared again. This time Helen and I scoured the marketplace and side alleys in vain and when we returned at half past nine we were both despondent. It was nearly eleven and we were thinking of bed when the doorbell rang.
>
> It was Oscar again, this time resting on the ample stomach of Jack Newbould. Jack was a gardener at one of the big houses.
>
> He hiccuped gently and gave me a huge benevolent smile. "Brought your cat, Mr. Herriot."

13. **distemper:** Infectious virus disease of young dogs.

### 2. Questions

Use your timeline to answer the following questions.
- What is the first event?
- What action do the narrator and his wife Helen take?
- What is the conclusion?

# USE VISUAL AND GRAPHIC CLUES

## Introduction

When you read, you can learn all kinds of information. Some information, however, does not come from words. **Visual and graphic aids** are pictorial representations that also help you learn about a subject. Visual and graphic sources of information include the following:

| | | | |
|---|---|---|---|
| diagrams | lists | maps | charts |
| illustrations | scale drawings | schedules | tables |
| timeline | graphs | cartoons | outlines |

One kind of visual or graphic aid that you may encounter is a line graph. Study this graph showing the mean temperature at a given location during the first half of August.

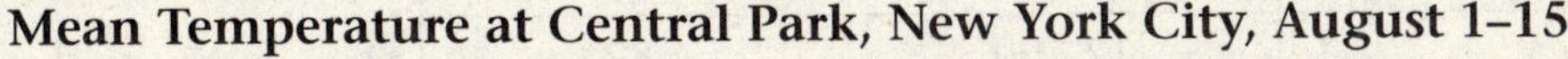

**Mean Temperature at Central Park, New York City, August 1–15**

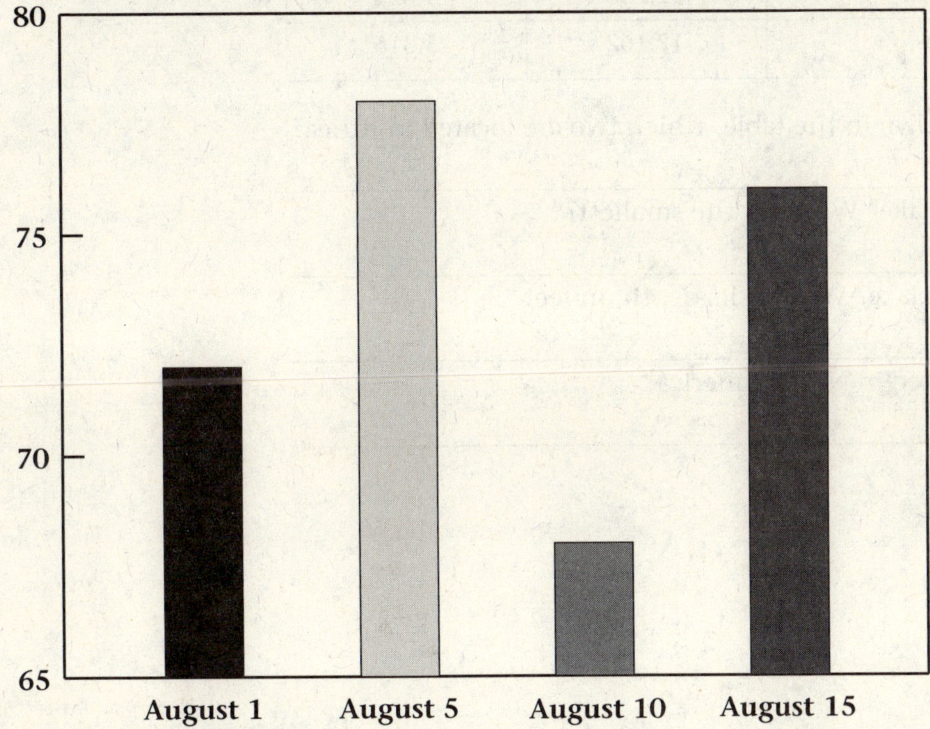



By reading this graph, you can tell that the mean temperature in New York rose between August 1 and August 5. Then the temperature fell over the next five days and rose again between August 10 and August 15. On what day in August was the mean temperature the highest?

**NAME** ____________________________________________  **DATE** ______________

## Practice

The table below shows facts about major natural lakes in the world.
Study the table and then answer the questions below.

| Lakes of the World | | | |
|---|---|---|---|
| **Name** | **Continent** | **Area (square miles)** | **Maximum Depth (feet)** |
| Caspian Sea | Asia-Europe | 143,244 | 3,363 |
| Superior | North America | 31,700 | 1,330 |
| Victoria | Africa | 26,828 | 270 |
| Aral Sea | Asia | 24,904 | 220 |
| Huron | North America | 23,000 | 750 |
| Michigan | North America | 22,300 | 923 |
| Tanganyika | Africa | 12,700 | 4,823 |
| Baykal | Asia | 12,162 | 5,315 |

**1.** Of the eight lakes shown in the table, which two are located in Africa?

_______________________________________________________________

**2.** Which is the largest lake? Which is the smallest?

_______________________________________________________________

**3.** Which is the deepest lake? What is its depth, in feet?

_______________________________________________________________

**4.** Which lakes are located in North America?

_______________________________________________________________

# ADJUST READING RATE

## Introduction

Every day you read a variety of different materials, from TV guides to newspaper headlines to the instructions on a test at school. You read some materials more quickly than others. The speed at which you read is called your **reading rate.**

You adjust your reading rate depending on what you are reading and what your purpose is for reading. For example, when you read a story for entertainment, you probably read fairly quickly. On the other hand, when you read a textbook or a magazine article to learn important information, you read more slowly and carefully.

Which of the following—a short story, a chapter about the history of a foreign country, or a grocery list—do you think you would read most quickly? Most slowly? Choosing the appropriate reading rate will help you get the most out of what you read. Before you begin to read, follow these steps to determine which reading rate is right for you:

1. First, consider your purpose for reading.
2. Then, look at the selection to find out how difficult it is to read.
3. Finally, decide whether you should read the selection at a faster, average, or slower rate.

The following guidelines may help you adjust your reading rate to suit your purpose and the type of material you are going to read:

- When you read to learn information or when you read difficult selections that contain unfamiliar words and ideas, read slowly and carefully.
- Read more quickly when you read for entertainment or when you read fairly easy selections about subjects with which you are familiar.

### Reading Tips

- Two strategies that will help you read more quickly and efficiently are skimming and scanning. **Skim** a selection to get a general impression about the topic. Do not read every word but look at the selection quickly, noticing the title, headings, words in boldface or italic type, and visual and graphic clues. Skimming a selection before you read will help you determine which reading rate to use.
- **Scan** a selection to find specific information, such as dates and important facts. Read quickly, moving your eyes over the page to locate key words that will help you find the information that you want.
- When you want to learn information and remember details, do a close reading. Read the entire selection slowly word for word.

## Practice

Below is a passage from "How the Snake Got Poison" by Zora Neale
Hurston. Before you read, skim the passage to determine which reading
rate you will use. Consider why you are reading this passage and how
difficult it is for you to read. Then read the passage, using the reading
rate that you selected, and answer the questions below.

> Well, when God made de snake he put him in de bushes to ornament de
> ground. But things didn't suit de snake so one day he got on de ladder
> and went up to see God.
>
> "Good mawnin', God."
>
> "How do you do, Snake?"
>
> "Ah[1] ain't so many, God, you put me down here on my belly in de
> dust and everything trods upon me and kills off my generations. Ah ain't
> got no kind of protection at all."
>
> God looked off towards immensity and thought about de subject for
> awhile, then he said, "Ah didn't mean for nothin' to be stompin' you
> snakes lak dat. You got to have some kind of a protection. Here, take dis
> poison and put it in yo' mouf and when they tromps on you, protect
> yo'self."

1. **Ah:** Dialect for "I."

1. What reading rate—faster, average, or slower—did you select for
   reading this passage?

   _________________________________________________________________

2. Why did you choose this reading rate?

   _________________________________________________________________

3. **Challenge!**
   Find three different types of selections that you are likely to read. (For
   example, you might consider a magazine article, a recipe, a bus
   schedule, an instruction manual for a video game, a short story, or
   another type of selection.) Skim each selection you choose, and decide
   at what rate you would read it—a faster rate, an average rate, or a
   slower rate. On a separate sheet of paper, explain why you chose the
   rate you did for each selection.

               

# ACTIVE READING: ACTIVATE PRIOR KNOWLEDGE

## Introduction

What you know before you open a book may decide how you react to it. Using the knowledge you already have about a particular subject can make what you read easier to understand.

In most cases, the subject of an article or a story will become clear to you once you have read the first paragraph or two of a piece of writing. At that point, you may want to stop and ask yourself what you already know about the subject.

### Reading Tip

Activate prior knowledge by asking yourself the following questions:
1. What is the subject of this piece of writing?
2. What do I already know about this subject?
3. Have I ever read about this subject before? If so, what specific details did I learn about it?

### *Model*

Read the passage below from "My Furthest-Back Person" (the inspiration for *Roots*) by Alex Haley. Identify the subject of the passage. Then quickly list a few things you know about it on a sheet of paper. Compare your answers to the sample list below.

> One Saturday in 1965 I happened to be walking past the National Archives building in Washington. Across the interim years I had thought of Grandma's old stories—otherwise I can't think what diverted me up the Archives' steps. And when a main reading room desk attendant asked if he could help me, I wouldn't have dreamed of admitting to him some curiosity hanging on from boyhood about my slave forebears. I kind of bumbled that I was interested in census records of Alamance County, North Carolina, just after the Civil War.

**Subject:** The author's search for his roots
1. What I already know:
   - Finding out about your roots involves doing historical research.
   - Since the author refers to his slave forebears, he is probably an African American.
   - Government buildings in Washington, D.C., contain a lot of information about United States history.
2. What I've read about this subject before:
   - I read a magazine article about the descendants of immigrants who traced their roots at the museum at Ellis Island.

**NAME** ___________________________________________     **DATE** ___________

# Practice

Below is a passage from "Nolan Ryan, Texas Treasure," by William W. Lace. Read the passage and then answer the questions that follow it.

Ryan's physical conditioning has kept him going long after most players his age have retired. He stays fit during the winter, and during the season, maintains a workout schedule of weightlifting, throwing, and running that almost never changes. The times are very different from his early days in baseball, when all a pitcher did between starts was throw enough each day to stay loose.

Mental fitness probably has been just as important. Even after 26 major-league seasons, baseball is still fun and challenging to Ryan. Yet, even though it's his living, baseball isn't his whole life. He spends as much time at home with his family as he can. He is keenly interested in cattle raising and operates three ranches in addition to his property near Alvin. He has many other business interests and spends much time on charity work.

The talented pitcher has not allowed fame and fortune to change his personality, as many star athletes have. Ryan remains what he always was—a modest, uncomplicated man from a middle-class, family-centered background.

"I still represent small-town Texas, and that's fine with me," he once said. "I'm still like the people who lived where I grew up. I've kept my roots. I'm proud of that."

1. Do you know of any famous athletes or film stars like Nolan Ryan who still seem to be modest people who have kept their roots? Explain your answer in a sentence or two.

   _______________________________________________________________

   _______________________________________________________________

   _______________________________________________________________

2. Why do you think it is important for a good athlete to maintain mental fitness as well as good physical conditioning?

   _______________________________________________________________

   _______________________________________________________________

   _______________________________________________________________

3. According to the passage, Nolan Ryan is a successful baseball player, but he also has other interests besides his career. Think of someone you know who is like Nolan Ryan in this way. Write a sentence or two about this person in the space below.

   _______________________________________________________________

   _______________________________________________________________

   _______________________________________________________________

# ACTIVE READING: KWL

## Introduction

**KWL** is a strategy that you can use to organize your thoughts before and after you read a selection. KWL stands for what you **know**, what you **want to know**, and what you **learn**. KWL gets you thinking about a topic before you read about it, and encourages you to ask questions that interest you and to try to find answers through your reading. A chart like the one below will help you to use the KWL strategy. Simply follow these three steps.

| Step 1 | Step 2 | Step 3 |
|---|---|---|
| **K**<br>(What You **Know**) | **W**<br>(What You **Want to Know**) | **L**<br>(What You **Learn**) |

*Model*

The passage below is from "Independence Hall" by Charles Kuralt. By knowing the topic of the selection or by reading the first sentence or two, you can complete the first two steps in the KWL strategy. Then, as you read, you can jot down what you learn. Read the passage and then look at the sample KWL chart to see how one reader used this technique.

> "I say let us wait." John Dickinson of Pennsylvania stood in this hall, July 1st, 1776, and begged the Continental Congress to be reasonable. "The time is not yet ripe for proclaiming independence. Instead of help from foreign powers, it will bring us disaster. I say we ought to hold back any declaration and remain the masters of our fate and our fame. All of Great Britain is armed against us. The wealth of the Empire is poured into her treasury. We shall weep at our folly."
>
> John Dickinson was not a timid or frightened man. He was a great old Quaker patriot, and he had a good argument. At the moment he spoke, British grenadiers[1] were sweeping down from Canada, British guns were bombarding Charleston, and just ninety miles away an incredible British armada was entering New York harbor....

1. **grenadiers:** Soldiers in a special unit of the British Army attached to the royal household.

| **K**<br>(What You **Know**) | **W**<br>(What You **Want to Know**) | **L**<br>(What You **Learn**) |
|---|---|---|
| • The Continental Congress debated whether or not to proclaim American independence. | • I want to know how the other members of Congress reacted to Dickinson's argument. | • The British were very powerful in July 1776. |

NAME _______________________________________  DATE _____________

## Practice

The passage below is from "Ribbons," a short story by Lawrence Yep. The story is about a family that lives in San Francisco. The children in the family are Stacy and her brother, Ian. The story focuses on the tensions caused by the arrival of their grandmother, who has come to visit from China. From that information, write down **what you know** and **what you want to know**. Then read the passage and complete the section in the chart for **what you learn**.

When I complained to Mom about how Grandmother was spoiling Ian, she only sighed, "He's a boy, Stacy. Back in China, boys are everything."

It wasn't until I saw Grandmother and Ian together the next day that I thought I really understood why she treated him so much better. She was sitting on a kitchen chair with her head bent over next to his. She had taught Ian enough Chinese so that they could hold short, simple conversations. With their faces so close, I could see how much alike they were.

Ian and I both have the same brown eyes, but his hair is black, while mine is brown, like Dad's. In fact, everything about Ian looks more Chinese. Except for the shape of my eyes, I look as Caucasian as Dad. And yet people sometimes stare at me as if I were a freak. I've always told myself that it's because they're ignorant and never learned manners, but it was really hard to have my own grandmother make me feel that way.

Even so, I kept telling myself: Grandmother is a hero. She saved my mother. She'll like me just as much as she likes Ian once she gets to know me. And, I thought in a flash, the best way to know a person is to know what she loves. For me, that was the ballet.

| K<br>What you **Know** | W<br>What you<br>**Want to Know** | L<br>What you **Learn** |
|---|---|---|
|  |  |  |
|  |  |  |
|  |  |  |
|  |  |  |
|  |  |  |

   

NAME _____________________________________ DATE ___________

# DISTINGUISH BETWEEN IMPORTANT AND UNIMPORTANT INFORMATION

## Introduction

Writers use a variety of details to discuss a topic or tell a story, and some details may be more important than others. By learning to distinguish between important and unimportant information, readers can focus on what is worth remembering.

Important information can appear throughout a piece of literature, not just in the opening and closing paragraphs. Study these steps that a reader can take to distinguish between important and unimportant information.

### Model

| 5. Explain why this information is important or unimportant. |
| 4. Ask yourself, "Should I remember this information?" |
| 3. Identify the details the writer gives. |
| 2. Decide what the passage is about. |
| 1. Read the whole passage. |

Use the steps to help you identify the important and less important information in this passage from "The Treasure of Lemon Brown" by Walter Dean Myers. Compare your answers to the ones below.

> Greg had sat in the small, pale green kitchen listening, knowing the lecture would end with his father saying he couldn't play ball with the Scorpions. He had asked his father the week before, and his father had said it depended on his next report card. It wasn't often the Scorpions took on new players, especially fourteen-year-olds, and this was a chance of a lifetime for Greg. He hadn't been allowed to play high school ball, which he had really wanted to do, but playing for the Community Center team was the next best thing. Report cards were due in a week, and Greg had been hoping for the best. But the principal had ended the suspense early when she sent that letter saying Greg would probably fail math if he didn't spend more time studying.

### Important Information

- Greg wants to play ball with the Scorpions.
- His father won't let him play because he is failing math.

These ideas are important because they show Greg's conflicts.

### Less Important Information

- The kitchen is pale green.
- Report cards are due in a week.

Critical Reading **STRATEGY**

## Practice

### Part I

Read the passage below from "No Gumption" by Russell Baker. Then fill in the chart.

> Brimming with zest, Doris, who was then seven years old, returned with me to the corner. She took a magazine from the bag, and when the light turned red she strode to the nearest car and banged her small fist against the closed window. The driver, probably startled at what he took to be a midget assaulting his car, lowered the window to stare, and Doris thrust a *Saturday Evening Post* at him. "You need this magazine," she piped, "and it only costs a nickel."
>
> Her salesmanship was irresistible. Before the light changed half a dozen times she disposed of the entire batch. I didn't feel humiliated. To the contrary, I was so happy I decided to give her a treat. Leading her to the vegetable store on Belleville Avenue, I bought three apples, which cost a nickel, and gave her one.
>
> "You shouldn't waste money," she said.
>
> "Eat your apple." I bit into mine.
>
> "You shouldn't eat before supper," she said. "It'll spoil your appetite."

| What is the passage about? | | |
|---|---|---|
| **What details are given?** | **Should I remember this information?** | **Why or why not?** |
| | | |
| | | |
| | | |

**NAME** _______________________________ **DATE** __________

## Part II

Read the following article about mongooses written by Gary A. Heidt for *The World Book Encyclopedia*. If you were preparing a report about the physical characteristics and the behavior of mongooses, which information from this article would you include? Which information would you *not* include?

At the bottom of this page, note the information that would be less important for your report. Explain why you would not include it. Then fill in the map on the next page.

> **Mongoose,** *MAHNG goos,* is the name of several closely related small animals that live in Africa and southern Asia. They are related to the civet and the genet (see **Civet**). The common mongoose is about 16 inches (41 centimeters) long and has stiff, yellowish-gray hair that is grizzled with brownish-black. It has a fierce disposition but can be tamed.
>
> The mongoose is best known for its ability to kill snakes. It is not immune to poison, but its swiftness allows it to seize and kill poisonous snakes such as the cobra. The mongoose also kills mice, rats, poultry, wild birds, and other small animals. It also eats birds' eggs.
>
> The mongoose has been introduced into Jamaica, Cuba, Puerto Rico, Hawaii, and other parts of the world to destroy hordes of rats. However, in most cases, the mongooses have done more damage to native birds than to the rats. Mongooses cannot be brought into the United States without a permit from the Bureau of Sport Fisheries and Wildlife. A permit is granted only if the animal will be used in a zoological exhibit or for educational, medical, or scientific purposes.
>
> **Scientific classification.** The mongoose belongs to the family Hepestidae. There are about 17 genera. One genus, *Herpestes,* includes many Asiatic mongooses.

### Less important information:

1. ________________________________________
2. ________________________________________
3. ________________________________________
4. ________________________________________

### Why?

1. ________________________________________
2. ________________________________________
3. ________________________________________
4. ________________________________________

**NAME** _______________________________________________   **DATE** _______________

## Part III

Fill in the center circle with your topic and the outer circles with
subtopics. Write important details on the lines. Explain your choices.

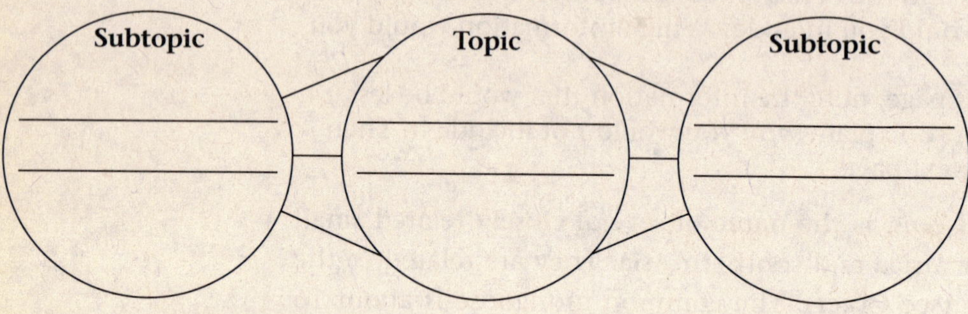


**Why I chose these details:**

_______________________________________________

_______________________________________________

_______________________________________________

_______________________________________________

_______________________________________________

_______________________________________________

NAME _________________________________________    DATE _____________

# DISTINGUISH BETWEEN FACT AND OPINION OR NONFACT

## Introduction

A text may contain facts, nonfacts, and opinions. In order to evaluate what they are reading, readers need to be aware of the distinction between fact and opinion or fact and nonfact.

A **fact** is a statement that can be proved to be true. Ways to prove facts include using reference sources, observation, and prior knowledge.

An **opinion** is the writer's personal feeling or belief. An opinion may not be false, but it cannot be proved to be true.

A **nonfact** is a statement based on guessing. It contains no evidence for proof.

### Helpful Hints

Readers can look for certain words or phrases that signal opinions. Examples of these signal words and phrases include the following:

| | | | |
|---|---|---|---|
| *I think* | *pretty* | *good* | *bad* |
| *I believe* | *attractive* | *wonderful* | *terrible* |
| *probably* | *ugly* | *safe* | *dangerous* |

### Model

The following paragraph from "Papa's Parrot" by Cynthia Rylant contains statements that express facts and opinions.

> The year Harry turned twelve was also the year Mr. Tillian got the parrot. He went to a pet store one day and bought one for more money than he could really afford. He brought the parrot to his shop, set its cage near the sign for maple clusters, and named it Rocky.
>
> Harry thought this was the strangest thing his father had ever done, and he told him so, but Mr. Tillian just ignored him.
>
> Rocky was good company for Mr. Tillian....

| Facts | Opinions |
|---|---|
| Harry turned twelve. | The parrot cost more money than Mr. Tillian could really afford. |
| Mr. Tillian bought a parrot. | |
| He named the parrot Rocky. | Harry thought this was the strangest thing his father had ever done. |
| He set its cage near the sign for maple clusters. | The parrot was good company. |

The statements in the right-hand column express opinions of the narrator and characters. Decide if this statement is fact, nonfact, or opinion.

Dogs are better pets than parrots are.

You're right if you decided that the statement is nonfact. There is no evidence to support it, and it may be proved to be untrue.

## Practice

### Part I

Below is a passage from "Stolen Day" by Sherwood Anderson. Read the passage and decide which statements are facts and which are opinions. Fill in the chart.

> It must be that all children are actors. The whole thing started with a boy on our street named Walter, who had inflammatory rheumatism. That's what they called it. He didn't have to go to school.
>
> Still he could walk about. He could go fishing in the creek or the waterworks pond. There was a place up at the pond where in the spring the water came tumbling over the dam and formed a deep pool. It was a good place. Sometimes you could get some big ones there.

| Statement or Idea | Fact? | Opinion? | Why? |
|---|---|---|---|
|  |  |  |  |
|  |  |  |  |
|  |  |  |  |
|  |  |  |  |
|  |  |  |  |
|  |  |  |  |
|  |  |  |  |
|  |  |  |  |
|  |  |  |  |

**Part II**

The following passage is from "Lather and Nothing Else" by Hernando Téllez. Read the passage and look for facts, opinions, and nonfacts. Answer the questions.

> And this was indeed a special customer. How many of ours had he sent to their death? How many had he mutilated? It was best not to think about it. Torres did not know I was his enemy. Neither he nor the others knew it. It was a secret shared by very few, just because that made it possible for me to inform the revolutionaries about Torres's activities in the town and what he planned to do every time he went on one of his raids to hunt down rebels. So it was going to be very difficult to explain how it was that I had him in my hands and then let him go in peace, alive, cleanshaven.
>
> His beard had now almost entirely disappeared. He looked younger, several years younger than when he had come in. I suppose that always happens to men who enter and leave barbershops. Under the strokes of my razor, Torres was rejuvenated; yes, because I am a good barber, the best in this town, and I say this in all modesty.

**1.** What facts can you find in this passage? How can they be proved?

_______________________________________________

_______________________________________________

_______________________________________________

_______________________________________________

**2.** What opinions can you find in this passage? How do you know?

_______________________________________________

_______________________________________________

_______________________________________________

_______________________________________________

**3.** What nonfacts can you find in this passage? How do you know?

_______________________________________________

_______________________________________________

_______________________________________________

_______________________________________________

## Part III

Read the passage below from "Heartache" by Anton Chekhov. Identify at least one fact, one opinion, and one nonfact. Give reasons for your decisions.

Evening twilight. Large wet flakes of snow circle lazily around the just lighted streetlamps and lie on roofs, horses' backs, caps, and shoulders in a thin, soft layer. Cabby Iona Potapov is all white as a ghost. As hunched over as a living body can be hunched, he sits on the box and does not stir. If a whole snowdrift were to fall on him, even then, it seems, he would not find it necessary to shake the snow off himself….His nag, too, is white and motionless. In her motionlessness, angularity of shape, and stick-like straightness, even up close she looks like a penny gingerbread horse. In all probability she is sunk in thought. One who has been torn away from the plow, from the customary grey scenes, and been cast here, into this whirlpool of monstrous light, unceasing din, and rushing people, cannot help thinking….

| Fact: | Reason: |
|---|---|
| _______________________ | _______________________ |
| _______________________ | _______________________ |
| _______________________ | _______________________ |

| Opinion: | Reason: |
|---|---|
| _______________________ | _______________________ |
| _______________________ | _______________________ |
| _______________________ | _______________________ |

| Nonfact: | Reason: |
|---|---|
| _______________________ | _______________________ |
| _______________________ | _______________________ |
| _______________________ | _______________________ |

**NAME** _______________________________________________   **DATE** ___________

# EVALUATE AUTHOR'S PURPOSE AND POINT OF VIEW

## Introduction

What different kinds of written materials—newspaper articles, travel brochures, recipes, magazine ads, instruction manuals, stories, postcards, speeches, textbook chapters, or poems—have you read this week? For what purpose was each of these pieces written? An **author's purpose** is the main reason that he or she has for writing.

An author's purpose may be one of the following:

|              |             |
|--------------|-------------|
| to entertain | to persuade |
| to describe  | to inform   |

For example, an author's main reason for writing a play or a story is to entertain. A travel brochure about an amusement park is written to describe, and a newspaper editorial is written to persuade. An author's purpose in writing an instruction manual is to inform. Being able to recognize why an author wrote a particular piece will help you to determine how you will read it and to appreciate what you read better.

The perspective an author takes when writing is called **point of view.** When you read nonfiction, or factual writing about real people, places, and events, the author's point of view is his or her opinions or attitudes toward a subject. By reading a selection carefully and by noting details, you can draw conclusions about an author's ideas and feelings.

When you read fiction, or writing about imaginary people, places, and events, the story is told from the point of view of an imaginary character. An author may tell a story from first-person or third-person point of view. The chart below shows the differences between these points of view.

| First Person | Third Person |
|---|---|
| A character in the story tells what happens, using the pronouns *I*, *me*, and *we*. | A narrator who is not one of the characters in the story tells what happens, using the pronouns *he*, *she*, and *it*. |

**NAME** ______________________________________  **DATE** ____________

# Practice

**A.** Read the passage below from "Winslow Homer: America's Greatest Painter," an essay by H. N. Levitt. Then complete the sentences that follow.

In a few short years, Homer's Civil War paintings brought him fame at home and abroad. He painted war as no other artist ever had. He emphasized not brutality but rather scenes of loneliness, camp life, endless waiting, and even horseplay on the battlefield.

Homer was a Yankee,[3] but he showed equal concern for soldiers from both the North and South. His paintings did not glorify war; they seemed to cry out for it to end.

His *Prisoners from the Front* made a reputation overnight. This one painting, done in Homer's honest, realistic style, showed the common humanity that linked North and South, victor and vanquished, Americans all. Homer's war paintings give us the best record we have of how the Civil War soldier actually looked and acted.

---

3. **Yankee:** Native or inhabitant of a northern state.

1. The author's purpose is ______________________________________

______________________________________________________________

2. The point of view is ______________________________________

______________________________________________________________

**B. Challenge!**
Complete the chart below. List three different works of fiction or nonfiction that you have recently read. Then identify the author's purpose and point of view.

| What I Have Read | Author's Purpose | Point of View |
|---|---|---|
|  |  |  |
|  |  |  |
|  |  |  |

NAME _______________________________     DATE __________

# DRAW CONCLUSIONS

## Introduction

**Drawing conclusions** means making judgments about what has
happened or what you have learned in your reading. Writers usually lead
the reader to a conclusion by arranging their facts in an orderly way.
When you read, use a diagram like the following to keep track of the
facts and the conclusions you can draw from them.

| Supporting Facts |
| --- |
| ________________________________________ |
| ________________________________________ |
| **Conclusion** |
| ________________________________________ |
| ________________________________________ |

### Model

What conclusions can you draw from the supporting facts in this
passage from "Suzy and Leah" by Jane Yolen? Compare your answers to
the ones below.

August 5, 1944

*Dear Diary,*

Today I walked past *that* place, the one that was in the newspaper, the one
all the kids have been talking about. Gosh, is it ugly! A line of rickety wooden
buildings just like in the army. And a fence lots higher than my head. With
barbed wire[1] on top. How can anyone—even a refugee—live there?

I took two candy bars along, just like everyone said I should. When I
held them up, all those kids just swarmed over to the fence, grabbing.
Like in a zoo. Except for this one girl, with two dark braids and bangs nearly
covering her eyes. She was just standing to one side, staring at me. It was
so creepy. After a minute I looked away. When I looked back, she was gone.
I mean gone. Disappeared as if she'd never been.

*Suzy*

_______________

1. **barbed wire:** Twisted wire with sharp points all along it, used for fences and barriers.

1. Supporting Facts: The buildings are ugly and rickety, with barbed-
   wire fences.
   Conclusion: Life in the refugee camp is hard.
2. Supporting Facts: Suzy notices a girl with two dark braids and bangs.
   The girl just stares at her. Suddenly the girl disappears.
   Conclusion: The strange girl has made a big impression on Suzy.

                    Draw Conclusions     **67**

## Practice

### Part I

Below is a passage from "Cat on the Go" by James Herriot. The passage is followed by three conclusions. List the supporting facts above the conclusions that are correct and cross out the conclusions that are wrong.

> It was as though Oscar's animal instinct told him he had to move as little as possible because he lay absolutely still day after day and looked up at us—and purred.
>
> His purr became part of our lives and when he eventually left his bed, sauntered through to our kitchen and began to sample Sam's dinner of meat and biscuit it was a moment of triumph. And I didn't spoil it by wondering if he was ready for solid food; I felt he knew.
>
> From then on it was sheer joy to watch the furry scarecrow fill out and grow strong, and as he ate and ate and the flesh spread over his bones the true beauty of his coat showed in the glossy medley of auburn, black and gold. We had a handsome cat on our hands.
>
> Once Oscar had fully recovered, Tristan was a regular visitor.
>
> He probably felt, and rightly, that he, more than I, had saved Oscar's life in the first place and he used to play with him for long periods. His favorite ploy was to push his leg round the corner of the table and withdraw it repeatedly just as the cat pawed at it.

**1.** Supporting Facts:_________________________________________

_________________________________________________________

Conclusion: Oscar the cat had been very ill.

**2.** Supporting Facts:_________________________________________

_________________________________________________________

Conclusion: Tristan did not especially like Oscar.

**3.** Supporting Facts:_________________________________________

_________________________________________________________

Conclusion: Oscar was a handsome cat.

NAME ___________________________________________   DATE ___________

**Part II**

Below is a passage from *Into Thin Air* by Jon Krakauer. Read the passage and then answer the questions that follow.

> The glacier's continual and often violent state of flux added an element of uncertainty to every ladder crossing. As the glacier moved, crevasses would sometimes compress, buckling ladders like toothpicks; other times a crevasse might expand, leaving a ladder dangling in the air, only tenuously supported, with neither end mounted on solid ice. Anchors securing the ladders and lines routinely melted out when the afternoon sun warmed the surrounding ice and snow. Despite daily maintenance, there was a very real danger that any given rope might pull loose under body weight.

1. What conclusion can you draw about mountain climbing from this passage?

   _______________________________________________________________

   _______________________________________________________________

2 List three facts from this passage that support the conclusion you have drawn.

   a. ____________________________________________________________

   _______________________________________________________________

   _______________________________________________________________

   b ____________________________________________________________

   _______________________________________________________________

   _______________________________________________________________

   c. ____________________________________________________________

   _______________________________________________________________

   _______________________________________________________________

**NAME** _______________________________   **DATE** ___________

## Part III

Below is a passage from "Ribbons" by Laurence Yep. The narrator, who is
a girl named Stacy, is talking with her mother about Grandmother Paw-
paw, who is on a visit from China. Read the passage and then answer the
questions that follow.

> Mom's forehead furrowed as if she wasn't sure how to explain things.
> "There was a time back in China when people thought women's feet had
> to be shaped a certain way to look beautiful. When a girl was about five,
> her mother would gradually bend her toes under the sole of her foot."
>
> "Ugh." Just thinking about it made my own feet ache. "Her own mother
> did that to her?"
>
> Mom smiled apologetically. "Her mother and father thought it would
> make their little girl attractive so she could marry a rich man. They were
> still doing it in some of the back areas of China long after it was outlawed
> in the rest of the country."
>
> ...
>
> Mom began to brush my hair with quick, light strokes. "The ribbons
> kept the blood from circulating freely and bringing more feeling to her
> feet. Once the ribbons were gone, her feet ached. They probably still do."
>
> I rubbed my own foot in sympathy. "But she doesn't complain."
>
> "That's how tough she is," Mom said.
>
> Finally the truth dawned on me. "And she mistook my toe-shoe ribbons
> for her old ones."
>
> Mom lowered the brush and nodded solemnly. "And she didn't want
> you to go through the same pain she had."

Give one conclusion you have drawn from the passage about each of the
following characters. Under the conclusion, give one supporting fact that
backs it up. The first conclusion is filled in for you.

1. Mom
   Conclusion: Mom wants to help Stacy understand what happened
   long ago to Grandmother.

   Supporting Fact: ________________________________________

   ________________________________________________________

2. Stacy

   Conclusion: __________________________________________

   Supporting Fact: ______________________________________

   ________________________________________________________

3. Grandmother

   Conclusion: __________________________________________

   Supporting Fact: ______________________________________

   ________________________________________________________

    

NAME _________________________________  DATE __________

# SUMMARIZE

## Introduction

To **summarize** means to tell briefly in your own words the main ideas of a piece of writing. When you summarize, you can condense your ideas or those of the writer into precise statements and omit unimportant details. When you are reading, you can choose and remember the most important parts of the author's writing. When readers write or tell the "short version" of what they've read, they summarize it. A summary includes the author's main ideas but leaves out the supporting details.

### *Model*

Read the following passage from "Tenochtitlan: Inside the Aztec Capital," by Jacqueline Dineen. Find the main idea and supporting details. Think about how you would summarize this passage, and compare your ideas to the summary given below.

> The city of Tenochtitlan began on an island in the middle of a swampy lake....The city started as a collection of huts. It began to grow after 1385, when Acamapichtli was king. The Aztecs were excellent engineers. They built three causeways over the swamp to link the city with the mainland. These were raised roads made of stone supported on wooden pillars. Parts of the causeways were bridges. These bridges could be removed to leave gaps and this prevented enemies from getting to the city. Fresh water was brought from the mainland to the city along stone aqueducts.[5]

5. **aqueducts:** Large pipes made for bringing water from a distant source.

Here is a *summary* of the same passage:

The city of Tenochtitlan began as a collection of huts on an island in the middle of a lake. After 1385, the city began to grow, due to the excellent engineering ability of the Aztecs, who built causeways to link the city to the mainland.

**NAME** ______________________________ **DATE** ____________

# Practice

Read the following passage from "The Californian's Tale" by Mark Twain. Then answer the questions that follow.

> It was a lonesome land! Not a sound in all those peaceful expanses of grass and woods but the drowsy hum of insects; no glimpse of man or beast; nothing to keep up your spirits and make you glad to be alive. And so, at last, in the early part of the afternoon, when I caught sight of a human creature, I felt a most grateful uplift.

1. What is the main idea of this passage?

   ______________________________________________________

2. Name two details that give more information about the main idea.

   ______________________________________________________

   ______________________________________________________

3. Use a complete sentence or sentences to summarize the passage.

   ______________________________________________________

   ______________________________________________________

4. **Challenge!**
   Read the following passage from "The Night the Bed Fell" by James Thurber. Then write a summary of one or two sentences.

> It happened, then, that my father had decided to sleep in the attic one night, to be away where he could think. My mother opposed the notion strongly because, she said, the old wooden bed up there was unsafe: it was wobbly and the heavy headboard would crash down on father's head in case the bed fell, and kill him. There was no dissuading him, however, and at a quarter to ten he closed the attic door behind him and went up the narrow twisting stairs.

**Summary**

______________________________________________________

______________________________________________________

______________________________________________________

______________________________________________________

______________________________________________________

# PARAPHRASE

## Introduction

When you use your own words to repeat someone else's message, you **paraphrase** what they have said. Paraphrasing is a helpful reading tool. When you are reading, identify the main ideas and their supporting details. If you can tell a story accurately in your own words, it shows that you understand the meaning of what you have read. Unlike a summary, where the reader is concerned mostly with the author's main ideas, a paraphrase also includes details.

### Model

Read this passage from "Rip Van Winkle" by Washington Irving. Paraphrase it in your mind as you read it. Compare your paraphrase with the one below.

> The bystanders began now to look at each other, nod, wink significantly, and tap their fingers against their foreheads. There was a whisper, also, about securing the gun, and keeping the old fellow from doing mischief, at the very suggestion of which the self-important man in the cocked hat retired with some precipitation. At this critical moment a fresh, comely[44] woman pressed through the throng to get a peep at the gray-bearded man. She had a chubby child in her arms, which, frightened at his looks, began to cry. "Hush, Rip," cried she, "hush, you little fool; the old man won't hurt you." The name of the child, the air of the  mother, the tone of her voice, all awakened a train of recollections in his mind.

44. **comely:** Attractive; pretty.

### Paraphrased Version

The bystanders began to think that the old man was crazy and might do some mischief with his gun. At this critical point, a young woman with a chubby child in her arms pressed forward to get a look at the old man. The baby began to cry, and the mother reassured her child, calling him by the name Rip. Something about her voice prompted memories in the old man's mind.



Paraphrase    **73**

**NAME** ___________________________________________  **DATE** ___________

## Practice

Paraphrase the following passage from "How to Enjoy Poetry" by James Dickey.

> Part of the spell of poetry is in the rhythm of language, used by poets who understand how powerful a factor rhythm can be, how compelling and unforgettable. Almost anything put into rhythm and rhyme is more memorable than the same thing said in prose. Why this is, no one knows completely, though the answer is surely rooted far down in the biology by means of which we exist; in the circulation of the blood that goes forth from the heart and comes back, and in the repetition of breathing.

___________________________________________________

___________________________________________________

___________________________________________________

___________________________________________________

___________________________________________________

___________________________________________________

___________________________________________________

# FORM GENERALIZATIONS

## Introduction

Effective readers sometimes act as detectives. They look for specific clues in their reading material and put these clues together to solve the mystery of the larger meaning of what they have read. When readers do this, they form **generalizations**, or broad ideas on what might be true in the book, story, or passage.

To form generalizations as you read, look carefully for sentences that relate to each other. Then ask yourself if the sentences give you general information that might be true but is not directly stated. If so, you have formed a generalization.

### Model

Read the following passage from "Melting Pot" by Anna Quindlen. As you read, try to form one or more generalizations about the information in the passage. See if your generalizations agree with the example given below.

> Change comes hard in America, but it comes constantly. The butcher whose old shop is now an antiques store sits day after day outside the pizzeria here like a lost child. The old people across the street cluster together and discuss what kind of money they might be offered if the person who bought their building wants to turn it into condominiums. The greengrocer stocks yellow peppers and fresh rosemary for the gourmands, plum tomatoes and broad-leaf parsley for the older Italians, mangoes for the Indians.

### Generalization

Change is a slow but constant fact of life in America.

This sentence states the central idea of the paragraph.

### Supporting Information From the Passage

The butcher's shop has become an antiques store.

Across the street, someone who has bought a building might turn it into condominiums.

The greengrocer stocks many different kinds of ethnic foods.

This supporting information helps to illustrate the generalization.

# Practice

Read the two passages below. The first passage is from "Melting Pot" by Anna Quindlen. The second passage is from "If—" by Rudyard Kipling. Make at least one generalization about each passage, and support it with information found there.

**Passage 1**

> Drawn in broad strokes, we live in a pressure cooker: oil and water, us and them. But if you come around at exactly the right time, you'll find members of all these groups gathered around complaining about the condition of the streets, on which everyone can agree. We melt together, then draw apart. I am the granddaughter of immigrants, a young professional—either an interloper or a longtime resident, depending on your concept of time. I am one of them, and one of us.

1. Generalization(s)

______________________________________________

______________________________________________

2. Supporting Information

______________________________________________

______________________________________________

**Passage 2**

> If you can talk with crowds and keep your virtue,
>   Or walk with Kings—nor lose the common touch,
> If neither foes nor loving friends can hurt you,
>   If all men count with you, but none too much;
> If you can fill the unforgiving minute
>   With sixty seconds' worth of distance run,
> Yours is the Earth and everything that's in it,
>   And—which is more—you'll be a Man, my son!

1. Generalization(s)

______________________________________________

______________________________________________

2. Supporting Information

______________________________________________

______________________________________________

**NAME** _______________________________________     **DATE** __________

Read the following passage. Then answer the questions that follow. Write the letter of the correct answer on the line at the right.

> It was not the only disappointment my mother felt in me. In the years that followed, I failed her so many times, each time asserting my own will, my right to fall short of expectations. I didn't get straight A's. I didn't become class president. I didn't get into Stanford. I dropped out of college.

[Amy Tan, "Two Kinds"]

1. Which statement below best expresses the main idea of the passage?     1. ______
   A. I didn't get into Stanford.
   B. I didn't become class president.
   C. I failed my mother many times in the years that followed.
   D. My mother had many expectations.

2. How should the word *asserting* be divided into syllables?     2. ______
   A. as-sert-ing                  C. a-ssert-ing
   B. as-ser-ting                  D. assert-ing

3. What inference can you make from the passage?     3. ______
   A. The narrator was a very good student.
   B. The narrator's mother had very high expectations.
   C. The narrator did not apply to Stanford.
   D. The narrator was more interested in sports than in her school subjects.

Read the following passage. Then answer the questions that follow. Write the letter of the correct answer on the line at the right.

> We didn't immediately pick the right kind of prodigy. At first my mother thought I could be a Chinese Shirley Temple.[1] We'd watch Shirley's old movies on TV as though they were training films. My mother would poke my arm and say, *"Ni-kan"*—You watch.

1. **Shirley Temple:** American child star of the 1930's, she starred in her first movie at age three and won an Academy Award at age six.

[Amy Tan, "Two Kinds"]

4. Which word below rhymes with *would?*     4. ______
   A. cold          B. hood          C. mood          D. mode

5. Which word below does *not* rhyme with *thought?*     5. ______
   A. taught        B. sought        C. brought        D. drought

6. Read the sentence. Then choose the meaning of the underlined word. Write     6. ______
   the letter of the correct answer on the line at the right.

> Within two years King Uther fell sick of a great malady, and for three days and three nights he was speechless.

[Mary MacLeod, "King Arthur: The Marvel of the Sword"]

   A. disease                   C. vanity
   B. hostility                 D. disturbance

     

Read the following passage. Then answer the questions that follow. Write the letter of the correct answer on the line at the right.

> Earl's lecture, delivered at decibels with which Tiger was unfamiliar, centered on the theme that golf owes no one anything, least of all success, and that quitting is a flagrant foul, intolerable. Even golf's most prolific winner, Jack Nicklaus, was renowned in part for the manner in which he accepted defeat. Even when he was losing, when he was far removed from contention, he continued to grind, as if a U.S. Open victory hung in the balance with each shot. From Earl's lesson, Tiger learned the importance of behaving similarly if he wanted to achieve the same level of greatness.

[John Strege, *Tiger: A Biography of Tiger Woods*]

7. What does the prefix *in-* mean in *intolerable?*     7. ______
   **A.** not          **B.** into          **C.** around          **D.** again

8. Which of the following statements is a *fact* presented in the passage, rather     8. ______
   than an opinion?
   **A.** Earl delivered a lecture to Tiger.
   **B.** Jack Nicklaus thought a U.S. Open victory hung in the balance on each shot.
   **C.** Golf owes no one anything, least of all success.
   **D.** Quitting is a flagrant foul.

9. Which statement below is the best paraphrase of the first sentence?     9. ______
   **A.** Earl spoke to Tiger very loudly.
   **B.** Earl gave Tiger a strong lecture, telling him that he should never quit if he
      wanted to succeed at golf.
   **C.** Quitting is all right under certain circumstances.
   **D.** Earl wanted Tiger to play better.

Read the following passage. Then answer the questions that follow. Write the letter of the correct answer on the line at the right.

> Anyway, here's what happened at Grand Central. One night last summer I worked late at the office. I was in a hurry to get uptown to my apartment so I decided to take the subway from Grand Central because it's faster than the bus.
>
>    Now, I don't know why this should have happened to me. I'm just an ordinary guy named Charley, thirty-one years old....

[Jack Finney, "The Third Level"]

10. Which item below best describes the author's purpose and the point of view in     10. ______
    the passage?
    **A.** to describe; third person
    **B.** to entertain; first person
    **C.** to persuade; first person
    **D.** to inform; third person

11. How should the word *ordinary* be divided into syllables?  11. ______
    A. ordi-na-ry          C. or-di-na-ry
    B. ord-in-ary          D. ord-i-na-ry

12. Read the sentence. Then choose the meaning of the underlined word. Write  12. ______
    the letter of the correct answer on the line at the right.

And he complained at his lot, doing all the smallest tasks, not being allowed to help with the threshing and ploughing, being teased for being so little and frail and tied to Cook's skirts and fit for nothing but gathering eggs.

[Karen Cushman, *The Midwife's Apprentice*]

    A. curious          C. delicate or weak
    B. low-born          D. sensitive

Read the following passage. Then answer the questions that follow. Write the letter of the correct answer on the line at the right.

He braced himself. The pull came. His toes went taut in their ice-holds and his hands tightened on the staff until the knuckles showed white. Again he could hear a scraping sound below, and he knew that the man was clawing his boots against the ice-wall, trying both to lever himself up and to take as much weight as possible off the improvised lifeline. But the wall obviously offered little help. Almost all his weight was on the lifeline. Suddenly there was a jerk, as one of the knots in the clothing slipped, and the staff was almost wrenched from Rudi's hands. But the knot held. And his hands held. He tried to call down, "All right?" but he had no breath for words. From below, the only sound was the scraping of boots on ice.

[James Ramsey Ullman, "A Boy and a Man"]

13. When was the staff almost wrenched from Rudi's hands?  13. ______
    A. after he called down, "All right?"
    B. after one of the knots in the clothing slipped
    C. before the man clawed his boots against the ice-wall
    D. before Rudi braced himself

14. Which conclusion below can you draw from the passage?  14. ______
    A. Rudi does not want to help the man.
    B. The man does not really need Rudi's help.
    C. The improvised lifeline is made from Rudi's clothing.
    D. The hole is not very deep.

NAME _________________________________________________ DATE _______________

Read the following passage. Then answer the questions that follow. Write the letter of the correct answer on the line at the right.

> Ötzi carefully laid his belongings, including his beautiful ax, against the rocks around him. He lay down to sleep on his left side atop a large stone as the snow fell through the frigid air.
>
> Days later, when Ötzi did not appear, other shepherds, or friends from the village, may have come looking for him. If they came upon the spot where he lay down, they would have found only a blanket of snow.
>
> [Don Lessem, *The Iceman*]

15. What does the suffix *-ly* mean in *carefully?*                    15. _______
    A. state, quality            C. in the manner of
    B. the most                  D. one that performs a task

16. What conclusion can you draw from the passage?                    16. _______
    A. Ötzi did not know how to use his ax.
    B. Ötzi died in the snowstorm.
    C. Ötzi had very few friends.
    D. Ötzi was probably not a shepherd.

Read the following passage. Then answer the question that follows. Write the letter of the correct answer on the line at the right.

> When I am too sad and too skinny to keep keeping, when I am a tiny thing against so many bricks, then it is I look at trees. When there is nothing left to look at on this street. Four who grew despite concrete. Four who reach and do not forget to reach. Four whose only reason is to be and be.
>
> [Sandra Cisneros, "Four Skinny Trees"]

17. Which statement below best expresses the implied main idea of the passage?    17. _______
    A. There are four trees on my street.
    B. The toughness and endurance of the trees give me inspiration when I'm
       feeling sad.
    C. The trees are endangered and must be saved.
    D. I seldom think of the trees, except when I'm depressed.

Read the following passage. Then answer the questions that follow. Write the letter of the correct answer on the line at the right.

> The number of cattle on the move was sometimes staggering: once, Teddy Blue rode to the top of a rise from which he could see seven herds strung out behind him; eight more up ahead; and the dust from an additional thirteen moving parallel to his. "All the cattle in the world," he remembered, "seemed to be coming up from Texas."
>
> [Geoffrey C. Ward, "The Real Story of a Cowboy's Life"]

          

**POST-TEST**

18. Which statement below best expresses the main idea of the passage?  18. ______
    A. Teddy Blue was an outstanding trail boss.
    B. The number of cattle on the move was sometimes staggering.
    C. It was dangerous to move too fast on a trail drive.
    D. The biggest trail drives started out in Texas.

19. The herds that Teddy Blue saw are classified according to  19. ______
    A. their size
    B. the number of cowboys with them
    C. the price they would bring
    D. their location

20. Which of the following is an *opinion* in the passage, rather than a fact?  20. ______
    A. Teddy Blue rode to the top of a rise.
    B. There were seven herds strung out behind him.
    C. He could see dust from additional herds moving parallel to his.
    D. All the cattle in the world seemed to be coming up from Texas.

Read the following passage. Then answer the question that follows. Write the letter of the correct answer on the line at the right.

> With a sense of smell at least 100 times better than a human's, Junior can pick up the scent of an orange lingering in a bag amid an array of smells from laundry to cosmetics. Trained Beagles with a year's experience have a success rate of about 80 percent. After two years on the job, the figure jumps to 90 percent. When they make a find, the dogs are rewarded with a biscuit.
>
> [Susan Essoyan, "Nosing Around U.S. Borders"]

21. Which of the following statements best summarizes the passage?  21. ______
    A. Trained Beagles like Junior have a high success rate at identifying scents.
    B. Junior can smell an orange in a bag, even if the bag also contains laundry and cosmetics.
    C. After two years on the job, a Beagle's success rate climbs from 80 percent to 90 percent.
    D. Trainers have found that Beagles enjoy a biscuit as a reward.

Read the following passage. Then answer the questions that follow. Write the letter of the correct answer on the line at the right.

> He went to his parents with a proposal. "When Justin was younger, say five or six," says his mother, "he used to give some of his allowance away to help others in need. His father and I would donate a dollar for every dollar Justin donated. So he asked us if it could be like the old days, if we'd match every dollar he put into buying old bikes. We said yes."
>
> [Phillip Hoose, "Justin Lebo"]

22. From context clues in the passage, how would you define the word *donate*?  22. ______
    A. split          B. give          C. save          D. allow

**NAME** _________________________________________________ **DATE** _______________

**23.** Choose the statement that is the best generalization about Justin.          23. _______
    **A.** Justin was dedicated to helping others in need.
    **B.** Justin persuaded his parents to increase his allowance.
    **C.** Justin was a good businessman.
    **D.** Justin had more money than he needed.

Read the following sentence. Then answer the questions that follow. Write the
letter of the correct answer on the line at the right.

> Ryan's physical conditioning has kept him going long after most players his age
> have retired.

[William W. Lace, "Nolan Ryan, Texas Treasure"]

**24.** Which word below sounds exactly like the first syllable of *physical?*          24. _______
    **A.** pit        **B.** fizz        **C.** pill        **D.** phone

**25.** Pronounce each word below, paying special attention to the sound of the final          25. _______
syllable. In which word does the last syllable *not* sound like the last syllable of
*condition?*
    **A.** competition  **B.** situation      **C.** vision      **D.** petition

Read the following passage. Then answer the questions that follow. Write the letter
of the correct answer on the line at the right.

> "On the other hand, there is a luminary up in the sky that helps us for part of
> the month and leaves us in the dark for part of the month. There are nights
> when the moon shines and Chelem has enough light. There are other nights when
> there is no moon and Chelem is dark. Now, why can't the moon shine for us
> every night?"
>
>    "Why not?" wondered the people of Chelem, looking skyward and shaking
> their heads thoughtfully.

[Blanche Serwer-Bernstein, "Let's Steal the Moon"]

**26.** The word *luminary* contains the Latin root *lum-*, which also appears in the          26. _______
words *luminosity, luminous,* and *illuminate.* What is the meaning of this root?
    **A.** pale        **B.** burn        **C.** light        **D.** flow

**27.** What contrast does the speaker draw in the first paragraph of the passage?          27. _______
    **A.** between Chelem and other towns in the area
    **B.** between older citizens of Chelem and younger citizens
    **C.** between the nights when the moon shines and the nights that are dark
    **D.** between the sun and the moon

      

NAME _______________________________     DATE _____________

Use the table below to answer the following questions.

| State | Nickname | Population (1997) | Area (square miles) | Capital |
|---|---|---|---|---|
| Hawaii | Aloha State | 1,186,602 | 6,459 | Honolulu |
| Idaho | Gem State | 1,210,232 | 83,574 | Boise |
| Illinois | Prairie State | 11,895,849 | 57,918 | Springfield |
| Indiana | Hoosier State | 5,864,108 | 36,420 | Indianapolis |
| Iowa | Hawkeye State | 2,852,423 | 56,276 | Des Moines |
| Kansas | Sunflower State | 2,594,840 | 82,282 | Topeka |

**28.** Which state is nicknamed the Prairie State?     28. ______
    **A.** Idaho        **C.** Indiana
    **B.** Illinois     **D.** Iowa

**29.** Which state shown in the table has the smallest population?     29. ______
    **A.** Hawaii     **C.** Iowa
    **B.** Idaho      **D.** Kansas

Read the following passage. Then answer the question that follows. Write the letter of the correct answer on the line at the right.

*Harper's Weekly* offered Homer a good job, and he could have remained a weekly[1] illustrator all his life. But he wanted to work for no one but himself, so he turned the offer down.

Homer left New York to paint the war. He joined Gen. George McClellan's Army of the Potomac[1] as a freelance artist-correspondent. He painted scenes at the siege of Yorktown[2] and did many drawings of Abraham Lincoln, the tall, gaunt, serious president who was desperately trying to keep the Union together.

1. **General George McClellan's Army of the Potomac:** McClellan served for a time as the general in chief of the Union Army during the Civil War. The Union Army in the East was known as the Army of the Potomac.
2. **Yorktown:** Yorktown, Virginia, which Gen. McClellan occupied on May 4, 1862.

[H. N. Levitt, "Winslow Homer: America's Greatest Painter"]

**30.** Some of the information in the passage is important and some is unimportant.     30. ______
    Which information is unimportant?
    **A.** *Harper's Weekly* offered Homer a good job, but he turned the offer down.
    **B.** Homer left New York to paint the war.
    **C.** He joined the Army of the Potomac as a freelance artist-correspondent.
    **D.** Abraham Lincoln was tall and gaunt.